"The Sierra Club believes in action . . .

"And we believe that as a result of what we and other conservation forces have accomplished, the environment of the U. S. today is a little better than it might otherwise be. Yet we have clearly done far too little. We have tried, and sometimes succeeded. But we have often been outnumbered and shouted down.

"So now we are cheering. We are cheering at the sight of fresh reinforcements from the nation's campuses. And we are waving a new flag. It is this handbook. Take it. Use it. . . ."

MICHAEL McCLOSKEY,
Executive Director
THE SIERRA CLUB

ecotactics:

THE SIERRA CLUB HANDBOOK FOR ENVIRONMENT ACTIVISTS includes a comprehensive survey of the youth movement by Peter Janssen, *Newsweek* education editor; chapters on the use of media, population control, how to run a teach-in, innovating conservation curricula, a "rap session" between Congressmen and campus editors, and the need for a land ethic.

With an Appendix listing professional conservation organizations (Round Earth Societies), a bibliography, and an activist's checklist.

ecotactics:

THE SIERRA CLUB HANDBOOK FOR ENVIRONMENTAL ACTIVISTS

edited by
John G. Mitchell with Constance L. Stallings

and

with an Introduction by Ralph Nader

PUBLISHED BY POCKET BOOKS · NEW YORK

ECOTACTICS:
The Sierra Club Handbook for Environment Activists

Pocket Book edition published April, 1970

The following articles are reprinted by permission:

"Where Life-Style Counts, Who Needs Nature?" by Alan Gussow, ©, 1969, the Open Space Institute.

"Tips on Conducting Environmental Conferences," by Lee Horstmann, ©, 1969, Moderator Communications Inc.

"The Ecology of Revolution," by Tony Wagner. Reprinted by permission from WIN Magazine.

This original *Pocket Book* edition is printed from
brand-new plates made from newly set, clear, easy-to-read type.
Pocket Book editions are published by Pocket Books, a division of
Simon & Schuster, Inc., 630 Fifth Avenue, New York, N.Y. 10020.
Trademarks registered in the United States and other countries.

L

Editor's Note

ecotactics (ē-ko tak′ tiks) *n. pl.* the science of arranging and maneuvering all available forces in action against enemies of the earth.

There is this to be said about *ecotactics:* you won't find it in any dictionary—not yet. Give it time. Meantime, accept our definition. It's what this handbook is all about.

To maneuver earth forces against the enemy, the tactician first indoctrinates the troops. But the polemics herein are brief and early, for we already know that the earth is going to hell in a wastebasket, and what we really need now is to know how we shall save this earth, not to mention saving ourselves. So the second thing to be said about this handbook is that it is basically positive. And not only in an inspirational way. People still are in the habit of learning more by example than by exhortation. Thus, between the essays, you will find the examples—the tactical case histories, if you will, of a movement that is clearly sweeping the country. You will find, I think, at least as much about *what* people are doing, and *how* they are doing it, as about why they decided to do it in the first place.

As for the people represented here, let it be known that they are, in aggregate, very young. Of some 28 individual contributors, only two are over 40. More than half are under 30. I mention this for several reasons. First, since it is the earth environment that concerns us here, then youth must be heard. This is *their* earth more than anyone else's: they will have to live with it longer, for better or for worse. And perhaps it is also appropriate that we listen to and learn from young people now because they are the ones who currently seem to be making the most sense out of a very bad environmental situation.

The youth of our contributors has something else going for it—and for you: their ideas and materials are fresh. This is no anthology of tomes resurrected from the past, for most of our contributors have no past in print. In a sense, then, *ecotactics* represents the publishing debut of a new wave of environmentalists. It is to them—and to the colleagues who stand with them at the ecological barricades—that this book is dedicated.

> JOHN G. MITCHELL
> New York City
> March, 1970

ecotactics

The Sierra Club Handbook for Environment Activists

PART I
the scene

PART II
where the action is

8   CONTENTS

PART III
three activists

PART IV
the land

PART V
the law

PART VI
the media

PART VII
rapping it out

PART VIII
a capitol colloquy

10   CONTENTS

PART IX
the learning process

PART X
endpieces

appendix

Foreword

A few years ago, our friends in law school laughed at us because we wanted to "change the world." Young activists in the Fifties, of course, represented the silent minority. Their laughing peers believed the lessons of the Thirties and Forties had already exposed the delusion of Grand Causes.

But with the causes of the Sixties—civil rights, antipoverty and peace—activism became a less lonely avocation. Suddenly, students discovered they could make a difference—and they did, producing some profound changes in public policy. Now, as the Seventies begin, we face a crisis that affects everyone in ways some of the earlier crises never did. The ecology of Earth's life-support system is disintegrating.

A revolution is truly needed—in our values, outlook and economic organization. For the crisis of our environment stems from a legacy of economic and technical premises which have been pursued in the absence of ecological knowledge. That other revolution, the industrial one that is turning sour, needs to be replaced by a revolution of new attitudes toward growth, goods, space and living things.

A meaningful revolution must be engaged in at all levels. First, we shall need grand statements. The dialectics must include declarations of *environmental* rights, new statements of national policy and priority and redefinitions of the public goals. We shall need political action: new laws and institutions must be created, old ones disbanded and thrown out; and direct mass action: rallies, marches, teach-ins. Perhaps more than anything else, we shall need individual action. Each person must become ecologically responsible—not only as a consumer of the planet's resources, but as a procreator of its most prolific species.

The Sierra Club believes in action. It has long been our hallmark. As an organization, we concentrate specifically on political action to change public policy because that is how the lasting improvements can be secured in our society. Ultimately, those who care the most, those who believe deeply in a good cause, discover that it is not enough simply to protest the status quo. Protests can lay the groundwork, but in a mass society changes are made only when the controlling institutions are forced to make them through the political process. Awkward and slow as it is, this process is often the avenue to achieving results.

The Sierra Club has learned quite a bit about the political process since its founding in 1892. And we believe that as a result of what we and other conservation forces have accomplished, the environment of the U.S. today is a little better than it might otherwise be. Yet we have clearly done far too little. We have tried, and sometimes succeeded. But we have often been outnumbered and shouted down.

So now we are cheering. We are cheering at the sight of fresh reinforcements from the nation's campuses. And we are waving a new flag. It is this handbook. Take it. Use it. If the Sierra Club can ever be of any help to you on the battle lines, just let us know.

MICHAEL MCCLOSKEY
Executive director
THE SIERRA CLUB
San Francisco
March, 1970

by Ralph Nader

Introduction

For centuries, man's efforts to control nature brought increasing security from trauma and disease. Cultures grew rapidly by harnessing the forces of nature to work and produce for proliferating populations. But in recent decades, the imbalanced application of man's energies to the land, water and air has abused these resources to a point where nature is turning on its abusers. The natural conditions of human health and safety are being subjected to complex and savage assaults. Yet these assaults are no longer primarily aesthetic and economic deprivations. They are now threatening the physiological integrity of our citizens. They are exacting their insidious toll daily. During the past decade, this country has begun to show that it can destroy itself inadvertently from within. Surely, this capability must be something new in the history of man.

In taking the initiative against those whose myopia, venality and indifference produce pollution, the first step is to equate the phenomena to our basic value system. Pollution is violence and environmental pollution is environmental violence. It is a violence that has different impacts, styles and time factors than the more primitive kind of violence such as crime in the streets.

Ralph Nader hardly needs an introduction (but *ecotactics* is proud to have his). Author of *Unsafe at Any Speed,* the nation's foremost consumer crusader now directs Nader's Raiders in forays against the dangerous follies of bureaucracy.

13

Yet in the size of the population exposed and the seriousness of the harm done, environmental violence far exceeds that of street crime.

Why then is there so much more official and citizen concern over crime in the streets? Some of the reasons are obvious. Primitive crime provokes sensory perceptions of a raw, instinctual nature; environmental crime generates a silent form of violence most often unfelt, unseen and unheard. Environmental crime is often accompanied by the production of economic and governmental benefits: consequently the costs are played down, especially since people other than the polluters are bearing them. The slogan, "that's the price of progress," is more than superficially ingrained in people continually confronted by industry arguments that any pollution crackdown will mean loss of jobs. Another reason is that power and polluters have always been closely associated. The corporate drive to reduce corporate costs and invest only in machinery and systems that enhance sales and profits is calculated to inflict as social costs on the public the contaminants of corporate activities. The same is true for the lack of attention by producers to the post-production fallout of their products as they interact, run off and become waste. Pesticides, nitrogen fertilizer and disposable containers are examples of such fallout.

Governmental activity in sewage and solid waste disposal and in defense research has also burgeoned environmental violence. Deep-well disposal of chemical wastes by the U.S. Army near Denver led to earth tremors and small earthquakes as well as to contamination of the subsoil. The Navy dumps tons of raw sewage into offshore waters, and its facilities, such as the notorious Fire Fighting School in San Diego, throw off pollutants into the air. Vessels carrying herbicides to Viet Nam and other areas of the world could possibly provoke one of history's greatest catastrophes: Should one ship sink and should the drums containing the chemicals be ruptured, marine organisms for miles around would be destroyed, thus reducing the oxygen supply available to mankind. The transfer of these herbicides through food to humans is another specter, given the fantastic geometric progression of the concentration of these chemicals from plankton on up the food-chain to man himself. Municipal waste disposal practices are, for many towns and cities, primitive; and where waste is treated, effluents still upset the ecology of lakes, streams and bays.

To deal with a system of oppression and suppression, which characterizes the environmental violence in this country, the first priority is to deprive the polluters of their unfounded legitimacy. Too often they assume a conservative, patriotic posture when in reality they are radical destroyers of a nation's resources and the most fundamental rights of people. Their power to block or manipulate existing laws permits them, as perpetrators, to keep the burden of proof on the victims. In a country whose people have always valued the "open book," corporate and government polluters crave secrecy and deny citizens access to the records of that which is harming their health and safety.

State and federal agencies keep undisclosed data on how much different companies pollute. Thus has industrial lethality been made a trade secret by a government that presumes to be democratic. Corporate executives—as in the auto companies—speak out against violence in the streets and are not brought to account for their responsibility in producing a scale of violence that utterly dwarfs street crime. Motor vehicles contribute at least 60 percent of the nation's air pollution by tonnage, with one company—General Motors— contributing 35 percent of the pollution tonnage. Many companies respond to critics by saying that they conform with legal pollution control standards. While this claim is often untrue—again as in the case of the domestic auto companies that are in widespread violation of vehicle pollution standards—the point must be made continually in rebuttal that the industries wrote much of the laws, stripped them of effective sanctions, starved their projected budgets and daily surrounded their administrators with well-funded lobbyists. The same industry spokesmen who assert the value of freedom of choice by consumers fail to recognize the massive, forced consumption inflicted on consumers and their progeny by industrial contaminants.

Until citizens begin to focus on this curious relationship between our most traditional values and their destruction by the polluters, moral indignation and pressures for change at the grass roots will not be effective. Effective action demands that full responsibility be imposed on polluters in the most durable, least costly and administratively feasible manner. The social costs of pollution must be cycled back to the polluter so that they are prevented at the earliest stage of the production or processing sequence. Achievement of this objective —whether dealing with automobiles, chemical plants or municipal waste disposal systems—requires communicating to the public and to pertinent authorities the known or knowable technological remedies. Moral imperatives to act become much more insistent with greater technical capability to do the job. Too many of our citizens have little or no understanding of the relative ease with which industry has or can obtain the technical solutions. As a result, too often the popular impression— encouraged by industry advertisements—is that industry is working at the limits of technology in controlling its pollution. This, of course, is nonsense. Furthermore, an action strategy must embrace the most meticulous understanding of the corporate structure—its points of access, its points of maximum responsiveness, its specific motivational sources and its constituencies.

General Motors is considered a producer of automobiles. It is time to view that company (and others like it) not only in the light of its impact on the economy but of its impact on urban and rural land use through its infernal internal combustion engines, on our solid waste disposal problem through its lack of attention to the problem of junked cars, on a huge diversion of public resources through the inefficiency of vehicle operation and designed-in repair and replacement costs, on water through its polluting plants, on safety of passengers through unsafe design and on a more rational, clean transportation system through its historic opposition to the development of mass transit. As a corporate state with annual revenues exceeding that of any foreign government except the Soviet Union, GM's average hourly gross around the clock of $2.4 million makes it a force of considerable substance.

Very little scholarly or action-oriented attention has been paid to such corporations, 200 of which control over two-thirds of the manufacturing assets of the country. This state of affairs is due to the curtain of secrecy surrounding corporate behavior and the great faith placed by citizens on the efficacy of governmental regulations. Corporations represent the most generic power system in the country. As such, layering their transgressions with governmental controls without treating the underlying system of corporate power simply leads, as it has done since the establishment of the Interstate Commerce Commission in 1887, to the takeover of the regulators by the regulatees. This is not to say that government agencies offer little potential for disciplining corporate polluters. It is only to emphasize that the restrictive hands of industry power must be lifted before these regulatory agencies can be returned to the people. But now there are indications that a business-oriented Administration will further develop a system of subsidizing the control of corporate pollution through liberal tax provisions, permissive attitudes toward unjustified price increases, and more direct payments. Such techniques have proved to be highly wasteful and inefficient and require the closest scrutiny both as policy and in operation.

Citizens' strategies for effecting corporate responsibility are concededly primitive. This is an area for great pioneering, imagination and insight on the part of citizens willing to view the corporation not as a monolith but as a composition of different groups inside and attached to it. A partial list of these groups illustrates

the broad opportunities for finding access and bringing
pressure for change. The list includes unions, employees,
institutional and individual shareholders, creditors, pen-
sioneers, suppliers, customers, dealers, law firms, trade
associations, professional societies, state and federal
regulatory agencies, and state attorney generals. To
be sure, many of these groups or individuals are presently unencouraging prospects for helping one tame
the corporate tiger. But recent years have shown how
rapidly matters can change when committed youth are
at large with unyielding stamina.

Youth must develop an investigative approach to the
problems of pollution. It is one of the most basic
prerequisites. Not only must there be a close analysis of
corporate statements, and periodicals, annual reports,
patents, correspondence, court records, regulations,
technical papers, Congressional hearings and agency reports and transcripts, but there must be a search for the
dissenting company engineer, the conscience-stricken
house lawyer, the concerned retiree or ex-employee, the
knowledgeable worker and the fact-laden supplier of the
industry or company under study. They are there somewhere. They must be located.

Top corporate executives crave anonymity and almost
uniformly decline to appear at universities and colleges
to speak or exchange thoughts with students. This
reticence is a functional one from their point of view.
It perpetuates the secrecy, the detachment and the tight-
knit circle that is corporate America. It hides the quantity and quality of the decisions which pollute the
environment. To widen the arena of discourse and to
expose these top, often insulated, executives to the
urgencies of the times, a consistent effort to bring them
on campus should be undertaken.

This quest should fit in with the formal educational
curricula. The problems of environmental pollution and
their origins are challenges to almost every discipline
of the university, from physical science to the humani-
ties. The curricula must be made to respond to our
need for knowledge about the ecosystem. Formal course

work, independent and summer work can involve empirical research, even the development of new environmental strategies. Formal education—to have a lasting legacy for the student—should thus strive to combine the development *in tandem* of technical skills and a humane value system. Action for ecological integrity has to be viewed as a process of endless discovery. To map the terrain, one must cover the terrain. There is no manual ready to guide, only a world to discover.

PART I

---

the scene

"If we choose to be plagued by big nightmares, we are entitled to offset them with equally big daydreams."

by John G. Mitchell

On the Spoor of the Slide Rule

"When we try to pick out anything by itself," wrote wilderness wanderer John Muir, "we find it hitched to everything else in the universe." Thus did Muir, who founded the Sierra Club in 1892, become one of the first to define in 25 words or less what ecology is all about. At the time, perhaps, his simple eloquence was wasted on a generation that had devoted itself to the unhitching of North American species, including the Indian, and was now hell-bent on stoking the new fires of technology. Who but a bearded mountaineer, after all, had time to contemplate the adhesiveness of inter-relationships in nature? Who then—in good conscience and patriotic spirit—dared challenge the rapid evolution of a singular society that would produce 10 million Babbitts even before Sinclair Lewis could coin the name? Of milk cartons and motor cars there would soon be plenty—more than enough to inspire Stephen Vincent Benet to observe wryly: "We don't know where we're going, but we're on our way."

We Americans have been so busily on our way for the past 50 years that we have only recently discovered all things are indeed interrelated. We now know, for example, that the salmon on our dinner plate is inextricably hitched to the farmer's south-forty. The hitch, of course, is DDT. We also know there is a hitch be-

John G. Mitchell, editor-in-chief of the Sierra Club, is a former newspaperman and science writer for *Newsweek* magazine.

tween the sonic boom and the psychic development of the human foetus, internal combustion and the living lung, waste disposal and water shortages, bulldozers and spiritual blight. We also possess the frightful knowledge that many of the ancient hitches, the natural ones, the links in the chains of life on this planet, are coming apart. We have not picked at them, as Muir would put it. We have wrenched.

By no accident the words *ecology* and *economy* are semantically hitched themselves. *Ekos* (or *oikus*)— Greek for house—is the root of both words. Our *ekos* is the Earth. Between the atmospheric roof of air above and the lithospheric cellar of rock below is our house and home, the biosphere. It is the only house mankind will ever have, interplanetary explorations notwithstanding. And today this house is in a frightful mess. Man, the Master, sits amidst offal in the living-room, counting his short-term profits. Well, tomorrow's another day. We'll get to the housekeeping then. But in the United States, that kind of tomorrow never seems to happen. Some people are beginning to suspect that, due to a lack of interest, tomorrow has been cancelled.

The American pioneer, for all his outstanding qualities, was a dreadful housekeeper. First he clear-cut the forest. Next he planted his crops. Then he failed to understand why the land went stale with erosion. So he moved on, beyond the western hills, and cut again and planted his fields and once more failed to understand. Yet Americans still cling to the pioneer ethic—even in this new age that has carried mankind at last beyond the frontiers of Planet Earth.

In his final speech as U.S. Ambassador to the United Nations, the late Adlai Stevenson delivered a statement that may well stand as the most significant of the 20th Century. He said:

> *We travel together, passengers on a little space-ship, dependent on its vulnerable resources of air and soil; all committed for our safety to its security*

and peace; preserved from annihilation only by the care, the work, and, I will say, the love we give our fragile craft.

Stevenson was not, in the traditional sense of the word, a conservationist. Yet he was in the vanguard of those who recognize that the earth environment, like a space-craft, is a closed system, dependent on that great life-support apparatus of Nature, with its carefully balanced mix of sunlight, water, green plants and oxygen.

Since our *ekos* is a spaceship, then our economy must become a spaceship economy in which no resource can ever again be considered without limits, including the resource of man himself. But as economist Kenneth Boulding so correctly points out, the U.S. has not yet accepted this principle. We still pursue what Boulding calls the cowboy economy. Growth and expansion must be celebrated. Nature must be subdued. Wilderness must be regarded with suspicion, for it is idle land. Cut, plant, mine the land and get out. Westward Ho!

Westward to where?

The American Cowboy, 1970-style, cuts a different figure than his grand-daddy. This one wears a white collar and is the fence-rider of technology. He packs no six-gun. *His* holsters hold slide rules. The Technocrat-Cowboy tells us not to worry about anything. Nature, he says, isn't important anymore. Its gifts can be reproduced in a test tube, or by computers. And so we are promised a brave new world in which the cowboys will corral DNA, the building block of cellular life. Not only will man thus be made molecularly perfect, but the world's food problems will be solved. Out of the test tube will come protein *à la algae*. Yummy.

The cowboys, of course, cannot dismiss the relevance of human evolution. Man can adapt, yes. To a remarkable extent he has adapted to a host of unnatural stimuli: poisonous air, malodorous water, demoniacal noise, oppressive overcrowding, and invasions of privacy. In some cities, some citizens have adjusted so well to these urban amenities that they seem, at times, to be non-participants in the process of civilization. Some 38 New Yorkers in 1964 ignored the screams of Kitty Genovese as she was stabbed to death beneath their windows. No one even bothered to call the police. So man *can* adapt, to almost anything. But more than a few scientists are beginning to wonder: In adapting, at what point does man cease to be human?

Wisconsin botanist Hugh Illtis believes man ceases to be human when he totally loses touch with Nature. Illtis writes:

> *Every basic adaptation of the human body, be it the ear, the eye, the brain, yes, even our psyche, demands for proper functioning access to an environment similar, at least, to the one in which these structures evolved through natural selection over the past 100 million years. For millions of generations . . . any of our monkey ancestors whose faulty vision caused them to miss the branches they jumped for fell to the ground and failed to become our ancestors . . .*
>
> *We cannot reject nature from our lives because we cannot change our genes. That must be why we, citified and clothed apes though we are, continually bring nature and its diversity and its beauty into our civilized lives, yet without any real understanding of why we do so. We have flower pots and pedigreed pets in our homes . . . and even in our airplanes "puke bags" with green beech leaves imprinted on the side to make us feel better, to alleviate boredom or sickness by tending to our largely genetically based appreciation of natural beauty.*

The gene pool of nature is important not only to what *we* are but to what we may need to continue to *be* what we are. Nearly all organisms molded by nature over millions of years have survived because of the range of variability built into their genetic structures. Thus, as climate or some other natural condition changes, a species can draw on a genetic variant—and survive.

We speak of saving a species—the whooping crane or the alligator—because it is rare, or because one species has no right to destroy another. But there's another reason to save the crane or the alligator, or the ecosystems of the Big Thicket, the Everglades, or the Grand Canyon. Each species or ecosystem may hold for us the answers to biological questions that have not yet been raised—questions which, Nancy Newhall and David Brower tell us, man has not yet learned how to ask. Henry David Thoreau wasn't kidding when he proclaimed—and not too prematurely at that—that "in wildness is the preservation of the world."

In the cowboy economy, the opportunities for preserving unquestioned answers are disappearing fast. First, we are witnessing a rapid loss of unrenewable resources. Second, we are fouling our nest at an alarming rate and with a multitude of pollutants. And finally, on a global scale, we Americans are exporting our slide rule brainstorms, our double-edged sword of technology, our genius for destruction, to promote the most massive modifications of the biosphere since the last of the glaciers retreated 10,000 years ago.

The unrenewable resources in greatest danger of depletion today are not the minerals that we gouge from the earth but our fellow-travelers on Spaceship Earth, those furred, finned, feathered and chlorophylled cousins of ours that evolved from our common colloidal soup. From our present perspective, one wonders now why Noah even bothered to take aboard passengers in the Great Biblical Flood. Consider North America. Since the Pilgrims celebrated the first Thanksgiving, at least 22 species of mammals, birds and fishes have forever disappeared from this continent—which means, in most cases, from this Earth. They did not go the way of the Jurassic reptiles, by eating their own eggs. They were exterminated by man. And now, incredibly enough, with wolves, coyotes, hawks and other natural predators the bounty-hunter's prey, another 59 vertebrate species are threatened with extinction. The gene pool has been further emasculated by the axe, and now the chain saw and bulldozer. In the U.S., more than 80 species of plants are living on borrowed time.

Another great unrenewable resource that is disappearing in the U.S. is the land itself. New concrete is poured over nearly one and a half million acres of it every year. By 1975, the U.S. will be building 2.5 million new housing units annually, and half of them will be single-family homes on lots calculated by archaic zoning regulations to *waste* land. New residential living space alone will annually require a land area nearly half the size of Rhode Island. And new interior roads, not the big expressways but the little neighborhood streets that lead to the front door, will stretch out over 22,000 linear miles—*every* year. In a little more than a decade, developers will have poured enough concrete over New Suburbia to build a Walnut Street to the moon.

But why wait until 1975 to calculate the consumption of land by cars and roads and parking facilities? They already occupy more space in the U.S. than people do. In Atlanta, to cite just one example, the voracious motor vehicle has cannibalized 60 percent of that city's parkland. And the U.S. government, paying lip service to the need for mass transportation, still proceeds to extend the Interstate Highway System through wilderness and city alike. Perhaps the White House should be moved to Detroit. Perhaps the Vatican, too, with its curious attitude toward contraception, should be moved to Detroit. The late William Vogt once observed that the motor vehicle "has become an adjunct of reproduction and probably has had a significant effect on vital statistics since many of the 20 percent of American women who are pregnant before marriage . . . have undoubtedly been inseminated in automobiles . . ."

Though the modern cowboy might challenge Vogt's analysis of the auto as a mobile fertility lab, he can hardly deny the vehicle's major role in poisoning the air. Despite Detroit's less-than-best efforts to reduce vehicle pollution at its source, the number of cars proliferate faster than the contaminants can be contained. And that seems to be true for almost every kind of waste in our all-consuming, waste-high society.

About every four seconds, the U.S. census clock ticks off a new American. In his expected 70 years of life, he will contribute to the Gross National Product by consuming 50 tons of food, 28 tons of iron and steel, 1,200 barrels of petroleum products, a ton and a half of fiber and 4,500 cubic feet of wood and paper. All of this material will pass through or around the new American, eventually winding up as waste—100 tons of it, wafting on the breeze, bobbing in mid-current or, along with his 10,000 "no deposit, no return" bottles, ploughed into some hapless marsh, there to pollute both the land and the sea. Nor does any of this take into consideration the consumption and subsequent waste involved each time the individual American throws an electric switch to light his private *ekos* or to shave the stubble from his chin. Clean energy, it seems, is a thing of the past, of muscles and waterwheels and wind-in-the-sail. Energy today comes from fossil fuels, which darken the sky; from nuclear reactors that overheat rivers, and from the turbines in high dams, which bury the rivers behind them under accumulated silt.

From an environmental point of view, no power system today is satisfactory. Nuclear power plants, for example, were initially hailed as "air cleaners." Their development allowed utilities to retire old coal and oil-burning plants. But soon the "nukes" were blamed for creating a new kind of thermal pollution that pours waste heat from the fission process into rivers, causing, in some instances, massive die-offs of fish. To solve that problem (and come up with a more efficient power plant, to boot) industry is now striving to develop a commercially feasible fusion reactor. And one of fusion's byproducts is tritium.

Tritium, or radioactive hydrogen, is not found in nature. One man who wishes it weren't found anywhere is Frank W. Stead of the Geological Survey in Denver. "They can talk of clean power from fusion," says Stead, "but it's strictly a frying-pan-and-fire situation." The trouble with tritium is that no one yet knows how much of it man can tolerate. Though presumably not as dangerous as such other radioactive substances as Iodine-131, tritium does emit beta radiation. Also, being hydrogen essentially, it has an affinity for water, and can follow water into the cells of the human body. Some scientists, notably Dr. LaMont Cole of Cornell, warn that man already receives much unavoidable radiation from the sun and even from X-rays. Since there is no human threshold for radiation, too much tritium conceivably could cause mutations or malignancies in future generations.

The tritium threat comes not only from fusion reactors but from Project Plowshare and other "peaceful" uses of fusion explosions. Stead, for one, is worried about what could happen when the non-proliferation treaty goes into effect, making fusion explosions available to any nation that might happen to want to dredge a new harbor, or get into the mining business atomically. Without an international agency to monitor tritium and other potentially harmful nuclear byproducts, says Stead, "We can hardly hand these things out like firecrackers."

Caution might also be exercised—but isn't—in the disposal of some of the highly toxic wastes the U.S. is currently flushing into deep, underground disposal wells. Pickling acids, pharmaceutical and petro-chemical byproducts, poison gases and other toxins—down they go, out of sight, out of mind. In the U.S. today there are some 130 such wells, and a full third of them are less than 2,000 feet deep in permeable sandstone or limestone strata laced with aquifers that feed eventually into waters on the surface of the earth. Scientists warn that the acids and poisons poured into these wells rarely stay put. "Once it gets into the drinking water," says geologist David Evans of the Colorado School of Mines, "there's no way in the world you can clean it up. It may take 50 years to discover that it's on the march, and by that time, the whole countryside is poisoned for miles around."

While most Americans may be willing to run such risks, some Europeans are not. Southwest of Sicily, on the tiny island of Lampedusa, a party of Italian government officials landed recently to inspect the terrain for a new deep-well disposal site. In wrathful self-interest, the islanders drove them off by force. Later, a mainland professor commented that Italy might soon be forced to rocket its wastes into space.

Few of the world's peoples are as environmentally enlightened as the Lampedusans. After all, the U.S. and the Soviet Union made it through technology. Why shouldn't they? And so the undeveloped nations are taking a quantum jump into the 20th Century—a jump that has landed more than a few of them in a pile of ecological crises. Some examples:

• Aswan Dam, the world's largest structure of its kind, was designed to reap the United Arab Republic a multitude of socioeconomic benefits: doubled electrical output, a 25 percent increase in cultivated land, the impoundment of 32 million cubic meters of water otherwise poured by the Nile River into the eastern Mediterranean. But already the Aswan account is in arrears. Aswan's giant Lake Nasser, not yet full of water, is beginning to fill instead with silt. The dam is also impounding natural minerals essential to the web of marine life in the Nile delta: since its completion five years ago, Egypt has suffered a $7-million-a-year loss in its native sardine industry. Now there are reports that the delta shrimp fishery is also drying up.

• Even before Aswan, the damming of the Zambesi River in Central Africa brought similar results. According to one report submitted by Cal Tech's Thayer Scudder at the Conservation Foundation's conference on the ecological aspects of international aid, the Zambesi dam-builders had predicted that an increase in the fisheries resource would offset the loss of flooded farmland. As it turned out, the fish catch fell off after an initial flourish, and the lakeshore soon bred hordes of tsetse flies that promptly infected the native livestock.

• From Chad and the Sudan, ecologist Raymond Dasmann reports that massive water development, intended to stabilize nomad herdsmen, has instead destroyed the region's ground cover. Over-grazing, in fact, has drawn the Sahara south and turned parts of Chad and Sudan into agricultural wastelands.

Behind every ecological boomerang lurks the cowboy-technocrat. Not satisfied with the wonders he has wrought in Africa, he now eyes the Amazon Basin of South America. And what does he see? More dams, dams enough to create an artificial lake the size of East and West Germany combined, dams and dikes and canals enough to turn the rain forests into a hydro-electric-transportation network linking the world's greatest river with the Orinoco watershed. What the technocrat cannot see are the long-range effects of so massive a modification. A new inland sea in the Amazon, some scientists fear, might well throw the heat/moisture balance askew at the equator and inflict some rather vast and frightening effects on the world weather system. At the same time, stopping the Amazon's discharge of nutrients to the sea could destroy the Atlantic shellfish industry as far north as the New England Coast.

The other Grand Design is for a new sea-level canal to be dredged (by nuclear explosions, no less) across the Central American isthmus—at a point where the Pacific is higher than the Atlantic and Caribbean, 18 feet higher, in fact, when the tides are out of phase. Zappo! The cold Pacific floods into the warm Caribbean. Goodbye Gulf Stream. Goodbye bikinis at Key Biscayne. Hello, thermal underwear. Aye, *there's* a hitch.

So it all comes home again to the Great American pioneer ethic, to what one perceptive observer has diagnosed as a bad case of "frontier hangover." Still groggy after nearly two centuries of exploiting our own land, we now seek new exploitative challenges abroad—and if it can be done, the saying goes, do it, even as the ill-fated British mountaineer George Mallory had to climb Mt. Everest simply *because it is there.*

In his Pulitzer Prize-winning book, *So Human An Animal,* Rockefeller University microbiologist René Dubos cites Mallory's heroic statement as an expression of man's determination to accept difficult challenges. But Dubos offers his own challenge. "Dashing expressions," he writes, "do not constitute an adequate substitute for the responsibility of making value judgments."

Yet value judgments in the U.S. are essentially economic. Such a judgment has clearly committed this nation to a $1.5 billion program to develop the supersonic jet transport (SST), the 300-passenger, 1,800-miles-per-hour bird that will lay down a carpet of ear-splitting noise 25 miles on either side of its flight path. Once again, the technocrats have told us not to worry. "First time you hear the sonic boom," said Maj. Gen. Jewell C. Maxwell, the FAA's former director for SST development, "you might jump. But the 1,000th time you don't do anything." Well, neurological basket cases don't do much of anything, anyway.

During the balance-of-payments panic, General Maxwell toured the luncheon circuit with facts and figures calculated to make the Superplane sound like nothing less than a flying Ft. Knox. The sale of just one SST abroad, said the general, would offset the U.S. cash outflow for eight million fifths of imported Scotch. And with barely a mention of the sonic boom or its impact on both man and nature, Maxwell added that America had what it takes to get the jet off the ground. What did the general think it takes? "The courage of a riverboat gambler." Shades of the old frontier.

The real gamble, however, is on man's ability to recognize technology-on-the-loose before it is too late. Scientists increasingly warn us that the environment is much like the human body. Deterioration takes its toll slowly. There are certain degenerative diseases for which the causal relationships are hard to establish. And yet we also know that while human life expectancy at birth now extends to age 70 in the U.S. and other western nations, life expectancy after 45 may be somewhat lower than it used to be. Similarly, Lake Erie's life expectancy in 10,000 B.C. may well have been 10 million years. Today, at the current rate of pollution and eutrophication, some limnologists give the lake less than a century.

How long will it be for man?

How long, indeed, in this nation which allocates less than .005 percent of its Gross National Product toward environmental quality, which encourages ecologists to study lichens and water fleas instead of people and ecosystems, and whose elected leaders choose to substitute rhetoric for action? It is as if we had embraced Benet's folk humor as national policy: not knowing where we're going, but sure-as-hell, damn-the-torpedoes, full-speed-ahead on our way.

Economist H. H. Landsberg once remarked that "if we choose to be plagued by big nightmares, we are entitled to offset them with equally big daydreams." Perhaps we indulge too much in the nightmares. Down the dark tunnel we see the fireballs of a nuclear holocaust. Or the new ice of a glacial era brought on prematurely because warmth from the sun can no longer penetrate the spoor of carbon dioxide high in the stratosphere. Or the specter of too much heat if solar radiation should, after all, penetrate the veil of global pollution only to be trapped by its "greenhouse effect." And what makes these nightmares really big is that no one can know—at this time—if they'll ever come true. There is no certainty about the daydreams, either. In the light at the end of the tunnel, we see the recycling of wastes, the end of over-population, of famine and pollution, the preservation of the species. We no longer see Babbitts, but Muirs and Thoreaus who know where they're going. And everything wrenched apart is hitched together again. It's possible. But simply dreaming of it will never make it so.

by Paul Brooks

Notes on the Conservation Revolution

A "conservation revolution" may sound like a paradox. Today conservation is "in." Everyone does it lip service. With the advent of the population scare, it has even replaced motherhood as the safest of all subjects. This has its dangers as well as its advantages. It can mislead the concerned citizen to think that the values conservationists are fighting for have at last been generally accepted. It conceals the fact that the conservation movement, though it operates within the law, is in principle revolutionary. The younger generation understands this. They are embracing conservation as a worthwhile cause because, properly understood, it goes to the root of our social philosophy; it is, in the literal sense of the word, radical. "The most hopeful sign for the future," writes Rene Dubos, "is the attempt by the rebellious young to reject our social values." Certainly it is the most hopeful sign for the future of conservation.

A young conservationist today has important advantages over his predecessors from previous generations. He is working in a different climate of opinion. But more to the point, he is working from a solid scientific base. The science of ecology has quite suddenly emerged from the obscurity of academic studies to become a

---

Paul Brooks, a director of the Sierra Club and editorial advisor of Houghton Mifflin Company, is the author of the book *Roadless Area* and has contributed numerous articles to the literature of conservation.

household word. The interrelationship between man and nature that poets and philosophers have been writing about for centuries, that George Perkins Marsh elucidated in a monumental tome just over a century ago, is beginning to be generally understood in theory, if not yet in practice. Anyone who can read and use his five senses must be aware by now of what happens when man considers himself as apart from, and superior to, his environment. He needs little scientific training to understand, in broad terms, how our present predicament came about; and no amount of technical gobble-dygook by the apologists for environmental destruction can obscure the basic facts.

Obviously it is an advantage to know, to be aware. But how can we apply our knowledge? Out of any number of possible examples, I would like to take two recent construction projects that would have degraded the environment on a colossal scale, in the name of progress—projects that are immediately concerned with the "social values" to which Professor Dubos refers, and in which the philosophy of the exploiter and the philosophy of the ecologist come into dramatic conflict. They are, first, the recent plan to dam the Yukon River in Alaska, and, second, the proposal for a superjetport in the Florida Everglades.

Geographically speaking, the late Rampart Dam and the dormant but still-threatening Everglades jetport could scarcely be further apart. But they have much in common. Both are located in areas where the physical environment is peculiarly fragile, and where the social and economic pressures are almost irresistible: areas that have rightly been chosen for top priority in the Sierra Club's conservation program. Both projects were halted at the zero hour, when aroused public opinion slowed their headlong course long enough for scientific studies to be made of the ecological consequences. The Yukon is presumably saved; the fate of the Everglades hangs in the balance. What can we learn from the parallels between the two? Since they both threaten destruction on such a grand scale, the lessons they provide are perhaps easier than usual to absorb.

To start with, both Rampart Dam and the Everglades jetport were promoted as the biggest ever: the former would create the largest artificial lake in the world; the latter, 39 square miles in extent, would be the equivalent of four or five of our largest airports rolled into one. Thus they would obviously be for the greater glory of America. (Huge dams in Siberia were used as an argument for Rampart; the race for the SST and world transportation for the jetport.) And as one looks into the specific claims of the promoters, the parallels become strikingly obvious. Let us examine three of the most familiar:

1) *The project will immediately create new jobs and will be a permanent asset to the economy.* Rampart promoters claimed the workers would double the local population; jetport promoters predicted a brand new city of a million.

2) *The land is worthless.* "Search the whole world," said Senator Gruening's administrative assistant, "and it would be difficult to find an equivalent area to the Yukon Flats with so little to be lost through flooding." (One recalls his novel standards for land values: there were "not more than ten flush toilets" in the whole region.) Similarly the jetport site is "useless" swamp which invites, this time, not flooding but draining: "There is plenty of room out there," said the head of the local Port Authorty.

3) *It is the only site for the project.*

One can disprove these claims on their own grounds. First, upwards of two billion dollars of federal money poured into Alaska would indeed create jobs, but they would go to the trained construction workers brought in from outside, not to native people now on relief. In the long view, Rampart Dam could be a financial bust; there is no foreseeable market for so much electric power unless a substantial part of the aluminum industry moved to Alaska, which it shows no signs of doing. Similarly, the Everglades jetport, like Rampart, would make a few people rich. The promoters claim that it would eventually create a city of a million people in the middle of what is now a swamp. A population explosion is the last thing Southern Florida needs: it has one already. It also has periodic shortages of water. The effluents from a city in such a location would eventually destroy Everglades National Park, a principal source of outside income. In fact, the very things that now attract people to the area would be lost.

On the second point, far from being worthless, the Yukon Flats are one of the great wildfowl nesting sites in the Arctic; the Yukon itself is an important salmon river; the whole area contributes heavily to Alaska's fur trade. Similarly, the Everglades is a wildlife paradise; the ecology of the whole region, including the valuable shrimp industry, depends on its preservation; it is an enormous asset to Southern Florida, even in purely economic terms.

Finally, in both cases, better sites exist. Devil's Canyon on the Susitua River, already approved by the Department of the Interior, is a superior site to the Rampart on the Yukon, and would cause virtually no wildlife damage. A far less damaging site for the jetport is also available, on land already owned by the state. It is one of several possible alternatives.

But it is not enough to meet the exploiters on their own ground, necessary though it may be in the immediate emergency. Obviously conservation becomes a positive force only insofar as it advocates an entirely different set of values. There is no point in talking about the "good guys" and the "bad guys." Senator Gruening was not wicked in promoting Rampart Dam. As with the promoters, so with the technicians; they are acting as they have been trained to act. To the average highway engineer, a landscape is something to be cut through, as directly and efficiently as possible. For him, ultimate truth lies in traffic patterns, and the compound cloverleaf is the highest form of art. Similarly, a free-flowing river is to an Army engineer what an unlicensed dog is to a dog-catcher: his first duty is to impound it, or otherwise prevent it from running wild. Each agency that threatens the environment has its own justification for what it is doing. The highway builders quote statistics on automobile production to justify more and wider expressways. The Corps of Engineers cite a "cost-benefit ratio" to prove that the public will profit from another dam. The Atomic Energy Commission must test bombs in a wildlife refuge to keep ahead of the Russians. The timber industry must be allowed a larger cut in the national forest to meet an alleged shortage of timber. The strip-miners must scalp the mountains because that is the cheapest way to get out the coal. The pesticide manufacturers must help our farmers feed the world. And so it goes.

When the ordinary citizen questions these activities, big business and government agencies have a ready answer: call in the public relations boys and persuade the public to take it. When *Silent Spring* was published, the National Agricultural Chemicals Association did not attempt to deal with the hazards that the book had exposed. Instead it appropriated a quarter of a million dollars in an attempt to prove—unsuccessfully—that Rachel Carson was a hysterical fool. When, some years ago, the Atomic Energy Commission wanted to test the earth-moving qualities of atomic bombs, it tried to persuade the people of northwest Alaska that they needed a harbor—even after it knew that a harbor was unfeasible at that site. One heard serious talk of "conditioning" the public to accept atomic fallout. Now we are to be "conditioned" to accept the supersonic boom. This Madison Avenue approach to public policy is a logical extension of one of the basic myths of our time: "Leave it to the experts," we are told, "they are dealing with technical matters that you can't possibly understand." As Sheldon Novick writes in *The Careless Atom,* social and political issues that depend on technology "are effectively screened from outside examina-

tion by the public's—and in most cases the Congress'
—lack of facts . . . We have been given not information, but judgements propounded by experts." Yet it
has been proved again and again that the general public
is quite capable of understanding scientific facts if they
are properly presented.

Of course, experts throughout the ages have been
aware that they jeopardize their power by giving their
secrets to the masses—or even worse, by confessing
that there *are* secrets. This axiom is recognized today
by the military, by many federal agencies, and by all
successful African witch doctors. A few centuries ago
one risked one's life by translating the Word of God
into the vernacular. Today the word of the Expert carries a similar air of sanctity in our technological society.

For sheer double-talk, it is hard to match a self-styled
expert who is trying to conceal the facts—or rather the
lack of facts—on which he based his conclusions. And
as Barry Commoner reminds us in his book, *Science
and Survival,* "The military holds no monopoly on the
imposition of scientific secrecy; industrial competition
may have the same result." He quotes the opening paragraph of an article on the toxicology of weed killers,
supposedly written by an expert to enlighten the reader
and encourage further study. Listen to this:

> Many of the toxicological data underlying assess-
> ment of the risks involved by using them (weed
> killers) in practice originate from confidential, non-
> published reports placed at the disposal of the
> authorities concerned. Such data have not been
> included in the present survey.

The myth of the expert—fostered by secrecy, sustained by modern techniques of persuasion—is a priceless asset to the public or private operator who wants to
manipulate the environment and at the same time to
manipulate people to accept the results of his meddling.
The environment can't fight back but fortunately the
people can. The modern priesthood of the technicians

begins to lose its hold on the people as the latter become scientifically literate and able to judge for themselves. The bones and the feathers that spill from the medicine man's bag turn out to be only bones and feathers after all.

Once the layman understands the technical issues, once he has hacked his way through the groves of gobbledygook, he is prepared to make his own judgment on the values involved. It has hitherto been the great weakness of the conservation movement that it has seemed so often to be on the defensive: trying to stop something from happening. In any dispute, the burden of proof has been automatically assumed to lie with the proponents of conservation. But as conservationists become both more knowledgeable and more numerous, this posture is changing. The average citizen's right to a decent environment—for which trained advocates like Robert Yannacone of the Environmental Defense Fund are fighting so effectively—is a positive, not a negative, concept. It represents the rejection of existing social values and a substitution of a quite different standard, one which is at last being recognized by the courts. The conservation movement has in fact become a revolution, the aims of which we are only just beginning to realize. Through long and often tedious experience, we are learning to meet the exploiters on their own grounds. And we are also finding that the public—particularly the young—are prepared to accept a whole new set of values, a quite different concept of man's relation to the earth.

by Tony Wagner

The Ecology of Revolution

The institutions we have created are destroying the liveability of the whole world; and the young people know it. They may not articulate it well, but they sense it. They feel it.
—Senator Gaylord Nelson

The most fundamental question facing us today is whether or not life will continue on this planet. Too often, movements for social change are caught in rhetorical traps which are peripheral to the more basic issue of life and death. We may debate economic alternatives until we become cold and numb, but the undeniable ecological reality is that an unlimited, infinite growth economy—the economy of spiraling, mindless "progress"—cannot exist in a limited, *finite* environment for very long. In other words, what good does it do us to postulate alternative economic systems when we haven't come to grips with immediate planetary reality —the fact that we are rapidly running out of such daily necessities as air and water.

We may discuss alternative political structures until we are hoarse, but an understanding of ecology—which I shall define as "the science of household survival"— suggests that if life on this planet is to continue, the only sensible political structure is one which is based upon

Tony Wagner, a senior at Friends World College, is pursuing an independent studies program in human ecology.

local and regional ecosystems whose boundaries have already been defined for us. Using the San Francisco Bay area as an example: while movements discuss communism, democracy, and anarchy, it is clear to most ecologists here that unless some form of regional government is created soon—a governmental form which would be based upon the understanding of the San Francisco Bay as one ecosystem and thus one political unit—the San Francisco Bay will soon cease to exist. The problem is that every little township which has some access to Bay frontage thinks that its particular needs and desires are most important. They all demand more land for factory sites, new housing, harbor facilities, or an "improved" town dump. Thus each little town is in a great rush to fill their part of the Bay in order to increase land within the township, and consequently increase the amount of property taxes that can be collected. In the last hundred years, over one-third of the Bay has been filled. A study made by the Army Corps of Engineers states that up to 90 percent *can* be filled. Only a comprehensive regional government will be able to settle the question of whether or not the Bay *will* be filled. If the San Francisco Bay is filled in, the result would be a severe disruption of the natural balance of the entire region, posing an immediate and direct threat to the quality of life in the Bay area. Clearly then, the issue is life. The politics and economics of the question are secondary.

Finally, we can argue the merits of third party politics, coalition movements, and student-worker alliances until doomsday, but in the coming years, there is only going to be one meaningful alliance—the grouping together of people who are totally committed to the affirmation of all life on this planet; not only human life, but plant and animal life as well.

We should address ourselves to the discovery of the missing link in the Ecology of Revolution; we should try to answer a question which appears to have been lost in the shuffle and rush of the last few years. While many of us have contributed in various ways to the "revolution," we have forgotten to continue to ask: *revolution for what?* End to Oppression, Fascist Pigs Off Campus, and Self-Determination are all advertising jingles of the revolution, but what is behind them? Perhaps it is because this question remains unanswered in the minds of so many that Senator Gaylord Nelson considers us inarticulate.

The Yippies say Revolution For The Hell Of It. Progressive Labor demands Revolution For Power To The People. When we are asked what the revolution is for, too often we reply with abstract political jargon, if we answer at all. It's so much easier to say what the revolution is against. And when we slip into negativistic, rhetorical, blanket condemnations, we leave ourselves wide open to charges of "nihilism" and "advocating the destruction of society," thereby assisting such organizations as the FBI and the Senate Permanent Subcommittee on Investigations, which are on a witch hunt for bomb-throwing anarchists. The average citizen, when he hears J. Edgar Hoover talk about "this conglomerate of malcontents . . . engineering a drive to destroy our educational system," can only nod his head in agreement; his total experience with the revolution having been, perhaps, a two-minute film strip of police-student riots, played to the tune of "Fascist Pigs Off Campus," followed by a brief Huntley-Brinkley melancholy monotone on the problems of youth. John Q., having had this sole experience with the movement, and seeing the fabric of society seemingly so threatened from every side, lends his reluctant approval to the witch hunt.

Increasingly, it becomes evident that unless we begin to articulate clearly what the revolution is for in terms that can be understood by everyone, some of us may well be "burned at the stake." At the very least, the revolution will be tarred and feathered, and forever banned from the village commons.

In our guts, most of us know what the revolution is for. Indeed, Senator Nelson told it like it is: "The institutions we have created are destroying the liveability

of the whole world . . ." The revolution is for Life and
against Death. The issues were clear, for once, in the
April 3 Movement against defense research at the Stanford Research Institute at Stanford University this
spring. Their theme was: Research Life, Not Death! As
a result of educating and organizing around the clear-
cut issue of life and death, and avoiding the use of
violent tactics which confuse the real issues, the April 3
Movement had a fresh spirit much like the feeling of the
civil rights movement in the early 1960's, and enjoyed
a tremendous sympathy and following, both on and off
campus. They had more student, faculty, and community support than any campus movement in recent
years. It was much later that part of the movement
began resorting to simplistic slogans, rock throwing,
and meaningless disruption—playing the game of cowboys and Indians with the cops. Then the issue became
law and order and destruction of property; the focus
of attention of life vs. death was lost, and with it, almost
all community support.

In light of the particular Stanford experience, and
remembering the changed tone of demonstrations in the
last few years, we are faced with another important
question: why are so many young white radicals turning
to tactics of violence? I think the answer is simple:
many of us, if we are honest with ourselves, feel hope-
less—afraid that there will be no future. It is our growing sense of hopelessness and frustration which leads us
to resort to violence. But how can we possibly affirm life
by destroying it?

I believe that the only way we can create a meaningful
human future, and overcome our own individual hopelessness, is to concentrate directly on the issue of life
and death. It is only through actively knowing the
natural and continuing process of life and growth,
within us and around us, that we are daily reborn—
becoming life; thereby enjoying each day, as well as
feeling a rational hope for the future. This is the
ecology of man.

If the revolution is to survive the witch hunt and

develop into a meaningful and effective means of change, with the backing of the educated majority, and if we are to overcome our own hopelessness, then we must make the issues crystal clear: the primary question is not who is going to have the power, nor is it moral or immoral war, and it is not capitalism vs. socialism. The first question is life! The primary question is the recognition of an undeniable ecological reality, and its understanding, which dictates a "radical" political stand. The question is the re-creation of a total environment which encourages life and growth, rather than death and destruction. Quite literally, what we are striving for is the physical and psychic survival of the human species on this planet. Our politics and our economics must be secondary, nevertheless intimately related, to the real issue of life and death. This is the ecology of revolution.

Just how can we focus our attention more concretely on the ecology of revolution? First of all, many of us will have to become much more deeply acquainted with the "undeniable ecological reality"—the problems of over-population and environmental deterioration. Some of us will have to study ecology in great depth. We must learn concretely just who is destroying the quality of life on this planet, and how they are doing it. And we must begin to learn the workings of ecosystems so that we will be able to put destroyed environments back together again.

There are many specific issues which we can bring to the attention of citizens in local communities. The air that we all have to breathe; is it going to cause lung cancer? The river that flows through our back yards; how badly is it polluted and who is it poisoning? DDT on vegetables and in milk at every corner store? DDT in human milk; what will it do to everyone's children, not to mention our grandchildren? And who, we can begin to ask, is responsible for this incredible poisoning of our planet—more specifically, our own back yards, because this is one issue which affects every one of us immediately and directly.

We can have ecology teach-ins. We can have fairs in

city parks, which might include displays on pollution, street theater, and action workshops. We can, in a weekend, create mini parks of our vacant lots—participatory parks which would bring people together to create, as well as dramatize the need for more open space. We can demand that all high school science courses include some study of the immediate physical environment—how was it 50 years ago, how is it now, and how could it be? And, of course, we should try to bring the issue of environmental problems into local political campaigns, and support only those candidates who are aware of the deterioration of the quality of life. We should support only those men and women who will not only limit mindless expansion, but who will work for a habitat whose scale and quality is conducive to meaningful human life and growth.

We can initiate discussions with our friendly grocer and neighborhood pesticide dealer—talking to them about DDT, and its effects on the human body. We can question the city council about the city's garbage dump —where are they going to haul all that trash in five or ten years when the present dump is filled? What about the small plant on the edge of town—why don't we go and talk to them about all the crap that comes out of their smokestack, or that they throw into the stream?

In our personal lives, we should avoid food which is not organically grown, useless possessions which will soon break down or become obsolete, and goods which have more wrapping than contents. We should stop using detergents which will not decompose through natural processes. (Use only *biodegradable* detergents.) We should seek alternative means of transportation other than the automobile—the number one criminal in air pollution. We can begin, as much as possible, to create communities which are an active expression of our hopes for the future—small groups of people who are constantly seeking more meaningful individual values and daily activity which is more consistent with these values and aspirations, and who continually engage in dialogue with the larger community, in the hopes of expressing a possible alternative way of life.

Ultimately, we can begin to consider nonviolent, direct action tactics. When the larger community understands that it is all of our lives and our children's lives which are at stake, and it is solely expediency and the short term profit motive which permits the environment to be increasingly poisoned, then why not boycott the hardware stores that continue to sell pesticides? Why not prevent the garbage trucks from rolling until the city council considers the effects of dumping on the environment? And why not prevent the delivery of raw materials to that plant whose managers are so intent upon turning those materials into more garbage and poison?

The national-international priorities become increasingly clear from an ecological point of view, also. The planet's resources are limited: we cannot afford such petty and dangerous extravaganzas as war, armies, and the ABM, especially when, according to most experts, there will be constant and widespread famine in as little as five to ten years.

It seems probable that, unless we begin now, by 1976 or so, a president will be elected to office who will promise to limit population and clean up the environment by strengthening and centralizing the power of the federal government, and imposing harsh and arbitrary restrictions—in a word, instituting a totalitarian system of government in the name of the preservation of life.

There is only one earth. We must all direct our attention toward limiting its population, ending its exploitation, cleaning it up, and generally making it a fit place to live. We don't have enough time to find a replacement. And so the revolution must be an affirmation of all life; our individual daily lives, the life of our community, and our earth.

PART II

---

where the action is

"You can't be serious about the environment without being a revolutionary. You have to be willing to restructure society."

by Peter R. Janssen

The Age of Ecology

Since Woodstock, many American students have come to believe that they are entering a peaceful, loving, brotherhooding Age of Aquarius, in which the sound of music (rock, of course) shall be heard again in our land. But within this questing movement, tens of thousands of young people have turned their own love toward the earth in an effort to repair ravished landscapes, oil-filled harbors and over-crowded cities, to patch the gaping holes in the quality of modern life. For them, this is the Age of Ecology. And from Berkeley to Boston, they are demanding an immediate end to the war against nature. In fact, there is no longer any question that Environment is *the* major issue on many campuses. "At first," says Edward Thomas, a Columbia University graduate student who worked in Senator Eugene Mc-Carthy's presidential campaign, "students worked for civil rights—and got chased out of Mississippi. Then we tried to change politics and end the war—and got beaten in Chicago. Now a lot of us are turning to the environment. It's right here. It's something we can do something about. And—for a change—we just might win this one."

The ranks of the new eco-activists cut across old traditional social and political lines, bringing together such strange barricade-fellows as short-haired athletes

Peter R. Janssen, a frequent contributor to national magazines, is education editor of *Newsweek* magazine.

and long-maned hippies, the reactionary right and the revolutionary left. Polluted air and reeking rivers, after all, affect everyone. At Harvard, a conservation club joined with the radical Students for a Democratic Society to bring in a speaker who had worked for Cesar Chavez, the California grape strike organizer. The topic: How DDT affects grape pickers. Even the War Resisters League has shown environmental concern. It recently devoted an entire issue of its monthly magazine *Win* (circulation: 8,000) to ecology. According to one editor, *Win* "yanked ecology out of the context of pure science and used it to describe the ways that man relates to his natural environment."

Keith Lampe, a founder of the Youth International Party, is now editor of *earth readout* (ERO), a news service devoted to the "ecological emergency." ERO serves about 50 underground papers. "Everyone knows now the environment is sick," says Lampe. "And everyone has at the back of his mind an image that we're ten years away from wearing gas masks. But who's going to respond to it? Older people don't have the energy. They tolerate poisoned air, the breakdown of subways and telephones. The kids don't have to. They aren't tied down. They don't fear defeat economically. They are freer and more flexible."

Young people in the U.S. are becoming increasingly concerned—and responsive—for a variety of reasons. Some see the issue as nothing less than the survival of mankind; some see it as a way of attacking the economic and social systems. Others simply wonder where all the flowers went. Michael Rossman, a 30-year-old Berkeley writer and organizer for educational reform, views the environment issue as an extension of the drug culture. "Drugs," says Rossman, "have had profound cultural consequences. One of them is that kids are turned on to colors and to their bodies. Kids are starting to become conscious of their physical selves. The hippie movement is turning toward the care and feeding of the body, to natural childbirth, to a reinvestigation of ourselves as animals on the planet, rather than as a conquering, domineering man, distinct from the rest of the system." Rossman adds that the last five years have been frustrating to young people in this country. "The further we got into the problems of civil rights and Viet Nam," he says, "the more tangled and ugly they seemed. The country today is pretty tense. There's a deep yearning in everybody's heart for one good clean cause. What could be better than erasing pollution?"

California poet Gary Snyder (who is profiled elsewhere in this volume) says, students have taken up the environment cause because of "a number of things that happened together. An interest in Oriental thought, in Buddhism, in American Indians, in tribalism, in communal living." But Snyder warns that colleges which encourage environmental activism are going to have a tiger by the tail: "Because you can't be serious about the environment without being a revolutionary. You have to be willing to restructure society."

With such gurus as Snyder and Rossman piping the tune, the West Coast has clearly emerged as the heartland of ecology activists. One of the strongest and oldest centers is Stanford University. There, for example, Rolf Eliassen, a 58-year-old professor of environmental engineering, has been teaching a course on man and his environment for the last eight years. The first class attracted just 30 students; this year 300 were crowded into a room designed for 240. In one class project last winter, a star football player was drawing diagrams to describe a sewage treatment process. In another, a law student was figuring out how to take care of one billion pounds of garbage. "This class," says a senior in economics, "is the first time that I've gotten into anything rational." The Stanford course is frankly designed to promote action. "We talk a lot about politics," says Eliassen. "Faced with a bad environment, how are you going to improve it? Students know all the ifs, ands and buts when they leave this course, and they can use them constructively. We preach the gospel of hope as opposed to the gospel of doom. I don't want them just to holler and say doomsday. I tell the women, 'If you want more appliances, then you'll have to decide whether you want a power plant on this side of the river or on the other side.' I teach them to become involved."

At the University of Washington, activists are trying to educate the community. "A lot of people still think water comes from the faucet and food from the grocery store," says Terry Cornelius, 20-year-old president of the Student Committee on the Environmental Crisis. "Of course, they don't. They come from the environment." As part of its campaign, the committee is offering environmental awareness classes to Seattle junior-high and grade-school children. Other students are urging merchants to stop selling merchandise made from alligator skins and polar bear fur. Cornelius' advice to activists elsewhere is to generate "a communal feeling in your students." Many members of his committee, for example, eat together, spend hours rapping together at night and on weekends, and generally share "a whole togetherness, developing a feeling among ourselves, living with a little more appreciation of nature and its resources."

A University of Oregon student group calls itself Nature's Conspiracy. Last year it organized a march— 1,500 demonstrators wearing green armbands—to protest the proposed sale of timber along French Pete Creek. And 1,700 students—more than one-tenth of the entire Oregon student body—signed up for a course entitled *Can Man Survive?*

Such expressions of concern, of course, are not uniformly welcome. Even before the French Pete incident, one timber association prepared a report predicting that within the year hundreds of radicalized students would be lying in front of lumber trucks or even sabotaging offshore oil wells. But Roger Mellem, a sophomore and leader of the Conspiracy, does not expect quite that degree of militancy. "We'll wait a while before shouting 'liberate the ecosystem,' " he quips. "We'll give the system a little more time than just a couple of months. But not *much* more."

At the University of California at Davis, members of Active Conservation Tactics at first organized in the traditional protect-the-wilderness spirit, marching off to the redwoods, picking up litter along the way. One group of Davis students still attends hearings and writes letters to protect wilderness areas, but the emphasis has shifted to a Zero Population Growth caucus which brings speakers to the school, and to a third group which is trying to get anti-pollution measures on the state ballot.

Much of the action at the University of California at Los Angeles has been organized by students who believe such activities are relatively tame and therefore unproductive. Last fall a coalition of groups, including anti-war activists turned eco-freaks, staged a sit-in at the campus offices where recruiters from Olin Corporation, Monsanto and Ford Motor Company were holding job interviews. The students were protesting the companies' contributions to the DDT menace and auto exhaust pollution.

The action, however, is by no means limited to the West Coast. At the University of Illinois in Champaign-Urbana a new organization called Students for Environmental Controls recently organized a campaign to clean up the aptly named Bone Yard Creek, which runs through the middle of the campus. Some 150 students and friends waded right in, loading seven trucks with more than 60 tons of garbage, including credit cards, bicycles, grocery carts and animal bones. Simultaneously, the university created a new course, General Engineering 293, to study pollution in Bone Yard Creek.

Sometimes, the direct approach results in confrontation. About 40 students at the University of Texas in Austin started a Student Legal Organization for Protection of the Environment (informally known as The Chlorophyll Conspiracy) and staged an uprising when the administration started to cut down trees along Waller Creek to expand the football stadium. Scores of students climbed up into the trees in protest. They stayed there until the police, under orders from Frank Erwin, chairman of the university board of regents, ascended ladders to pluck them down. Twenty-six were arrested. A few days later, the faculty voted 242 to 197 to urge the impeachment of Erwin.

Protests often move off campus. Students for Environmental Defense at the University of Minnesota, for example, went directly to the source to protest the American Can Company's no-return containers. Wes Fischer, a 26-year-old Ph.D. candidate in ecology and the organization's president, dressed himself in a page's costume and accompanied two truckloads of empty cans to the company's offices in St. Paul. He then presented startled corporate executives with a golden can sitting on a red velvet cushion. Minnesota students also held a mock burial of an internal combustion engine to protest gasoline pollution. Some of the "mourners" held placards declaiming "Bury the Engine Before It Buries Us." Then, as the engine was lowered into the grave, a minister solemnly intoned: "For the sake of mankind, rust to rust." The activists gained notoriety for this imaginative production. "We do something slightly wild," Fischer says, "and then issue a straight statement of why we're doing it so the press can have a very clear explanation. The media go for this technique. They seem to look on us as the good young people of America."

Tactics that are "slightly wild" have also been tested in the Boston area. There, about 40 eco-freaks, mostly members of Boston's Ecology Action group, donned gas masks and marched down Massachusetts Avenue to the War Memorial Auditorium to demonstrate at the opening of the International Auto Show. The star of the picket line was a "victim of auto pollution." He sat in a wheelchair, wheezing through a gas mask. Ecology Action members also marched to the Prudential Center headquarters of Boston Edison and awarded that utility a big blue ribbon as "Polluter of the Year."

Columbia University's Ecology Action lives up to its name, too. Half its members are SDSers; the other half, according to junior Gene Nathanson, are "unpolitical freaks who are into camping, hiking and mountain climbing." Ecology Action's first move was to protest the building of a nuclear reactor. In keeping with Columbia's radical traditions, the demonstration drew 150 people in a heavy rain; they promptly launched a brief sit-in at the administration building. On calmer days, Columbia's Ecology Action tries to develop potential uses for nearby Morningside Park and conducts research in food additives. "Our main objective," says Nathanson, "is to get people to really think about how close we are to disaster. We're not interested in just staying on campus. We want to develop a consciousness toward possible solutions of the problems. In New York, that means housing and transit as well as pollution.

The University of Wisconsin at Madison, long a showcase of radical student causes, is now a center of environmental activity. And it is well organized. Some of the activity was seeded one afternoon when a friend asked Dennis Sustare, a graduate student in zoology, what his research project was all about. Sustare replied that it dealt with the thermal budget of spiders. "Now what the hell," the friend demanded, "is that going to do for me?" Sustare didn't have an answer, and soon decided that his academic research was irrelevant. So he and other students formed the Ecology Students Association, which is studying water pollution and waste disposal in the Madison area, as well as the use of defoliants in Viet Nam.

Other Madison organizations, including the more radical Science Students Union and the Engineers and Scientists for Social Responsibility, have started a course in ecology at the student-run Free University, helped establish a human ecology course within the formal university, issued position papers on various ecological problems, and presented a list of demands for action on pollution to the university administration. Madison being Madison, some students have formed a Whole Earth Cooperative, specializing in macro-biotic health foods. The co-op offers "the raw materials for healthy living within a polluted environment."

The most common form of activism, however, is far less eclectic, usually involving the distribution of educational or inspirational materials. The Environmental Action for Survival Committee (ENACT) at the University of Michigan has sold several thousand of its "Give Earth A Chance" buttons. And ENACT sponsors weekly community lectures using speakers from some 40 university departments, from architecture to zoology, to attract wide audiences from both the campus and the community.

At the University of Maryland, a school rarely rocked by student revolt, the North American Habitat Preservation Society is spurring on the environment movement by trying to persuade the state to hold Maryland's wetlands in trust for the public. The society also organized a campus "trash bash." More than 1,000 students volunteered to pick up litter from the campus and an eight-square-mile area around it. The city of College Park donated garbage bags for the cleanup, the university provided trucks, rakes and shovels, and the state disposed of the garbage. But the community's involvement was disappointing. "This community," says Doyle Grabarck, a 26-year-old doctoral candidate in biochemistry, "does a lot of pushing, but no shoveling."

The Maryland approach is moderate. Students are trying to work with local industry. "Conservation doesn't understand industry's problems," Grabarck says, "and industry has never taken the time to understand what they're doing to the environment. We have to communicate with and educate industry. We'll have to condemn certain of their techniques, and they'll have to do some self-condemnation. It may never work, but it's got to be tried. We're all an intricate part of the same world." Meanwhile, just in case the communications fail, Grabarck is producing vinyl bumper stickers proclaiming: "Pounce on Polluters."

The communications game has been mastered in Cleveland not by a campus group but by an inter-high school coalition called the Academic Council on Environmental Problems. Its monthly symposia on pollution problems attract a diverse cross section of community leaders, and its monthly newsletter, *The*

Waste Paper, carries the good word to some 1,000 readers.

Some campus activists have trouble establishing any valid line of communication with the community. For example, a group of students at the University of Arizona marched in the last annual Copper Days parade to protest air pollution from local copper mines. Their issue was not overwhelmingly popular. "We couldn't be too hard on the mines," says Jeffrey Kuchar, president of the campus Young Democrats and board member of GASP (Group Against Smelter Pollution), "or people would really not pay any attention. A lot of them depend on the industry. They're afraid we'll chase it away. Arizona is a real conservative state."

Where the lines of campus-community communication leave something to be desired, or where the hardcore activists are few, a college or university may still contribute to the movement through research. The Associated Students for the California Institute of Technology are now in their third year of pollution research. In an unusual windfall for student groups, ASCIT received a $68,000 grant from the U.S. Department of Health, Education and Welfare, and $42,000 from the National Science Foundation. The first grant was used in part to create a computerized car-pool for workers at a Lockheed factory. The idea was that if more workers rode to the factory together, there would be less auto pollution. About 2,500 of the factory's 10,000 workers took part in the car-pool, but the project had little effect on total auto emissions or on Southern Californians' desire to use their own cars. Another ASCIT project has studied what happens to a mountainside after a forest fire. One finding indicated that wax from burned chaparral shrubbery coats the dirt, allowing the water to rush down the hills in torrents of floods and mudslides.

The happiest combination of forces, of course, is one in which campus activists and townspeople work together. ECOS, a new environmental group at the University of North Carolina in Chapel Hill, is such a coalition. Organized by six ecologists last fall, without any publicity at all its membership grew from six to 30, and now includes faculty, undergraduates, field graduate students, and a strong representation from Chapel Hill's League of Women Voters. ECOS's first major project: "Responsible Contraception—Why and How," a four-day running panel staged at the Student Union by a physician, marriage counselor, and minister. ECOS also showed four films dealing with the population explosion, depicting the desirability of two-child families and some "pretty specific" methods of contraception. In addition, ECOS offered participants a mimeographed bibliography of 42 books on human sexuality, contraception and population.

The future of the student environment movement is uncertain. Keith Lampe of *earth readout* predicts that students gradually will become more radical in arriving at solutions to ecological problems and probably will embrace new and militant forms of politics. Lampe himself proposes abandoning national and state governments in the United States, Canada and Mexico, and organizing North America along natural and cultural lines, possibly into the original eight North American Indian areas with smaller divisions around windshed, watershed and other natural features. And Steven Beckwitt, 26, a regular contributor to *earth readout,* believes that students increasingly will adopt an anti-growth philosophy. "We're going to see a decline in consumption among the youth of this country in the next four or five years," Beckwitt says. "They realize they're essentially consuming their own future. This doesn't mean rejecting everything and living like a monk. But you just don't need to consume a new car every four or five years. You can keep the old one running for 20 years."

Still, some observers of the movement say the majority in it aren't radical enough to consume less, that "the kids don't want to revolutionize society—they just want to live in it." But the skeptics are wrong. To live much longer in this society, young people *will* have to revolutionize it. In fact, they have already begun.

by Cynthia Wayburn

Shaping up Santa Cruz

The 2,000-acre campus of the University of California at Santa Cruz rolls out under redwoods and across open meadows in the hills above one of California's most historic towns. It is a young campus, not yet six years old. The administration is receptive to experimental ideas, and there is a free exchange of them between faculty and students. The physical plant and the educational climate, in short, provide a unique environment in which to innovate *environment* activities. At Santa Cruz, students, professors and members of the off-campus community are beginning to take full advantage of the opportunities. Here's how it is shaping up:

Rapping with the community

Every Thursday, members of such campus organizations as Ecology Action and Zero Population gather for lunch at one of the university's dining hall annexes. Our guests include members of the faculty, students interested in environmental affairs, and visitors from the surrounding community. We try to involve these guests from the community in our projects. We tell them what worries us in terms of the immediate environment. And we tell them what we plan to do about the things that bother us. Through these luncheons we keep the lines

Cynthia Wayburn, an active environmentalist, is a senior at the University of California at Santa Cruz.

of communication open. Once, the university's chancellor joined us, and before long we expect to be lunching with a Santa Cruz County supervisor. The dialogues that develop during these lunches are mutually beneficial. They keep us thinking, and innovating.

Recycling wastes

We at Santa Cruz have persuaded the chancellor that it would be in the university's best interests to recycle its waste paper. We explained to the chancellor that the State of California—of which the university is, of course, a part—already has a contract for disposal of waste paper with a firm that re-uses the waste. Our argument was based largely on economics: the university presently spends five dollars a ton for disposal; it could be making $11.18 a ton, under the terms of the contract, by selling the waste paper to the recycling firm.

The university will soon be recycling aluminum cans as well. Reynolds Aluminum Company is already accepting the empties. The company pays half a cent apiece for them—even more when returned in bulk. Reynolds plans to open a recycling plant in Hayward, California, approximately 70 miles from Santa Cruz, sometime this year. Meanwhile, students are setting up special collection bins next to all the soft drink machines on campus.

Master planning

A re-evaluation of the campus master plan has been undertaken by a graduate student. Working with other students and professors, the post-grad is targeting in on the university's transportation system. People are eager to keep additional cars off campus, and there is now support for a proposal to create off-campus parking facilities and non-polluting alternatives to the auto on campus. Our suggested alternative: a steam monorail.

Students are also studying a five-mile stretch of the Pacific Coast north of Santa Cruz. They hope to inventory the area's natural values, define its dwindling resources, and then present their findings to county officials with special recommendations for shoreline protection.

Spreading the word

In an effort to bring environmental awareness to as many people as possible, regardless of their intellectual backgrounds, we are in the process of outlining an interdisciplinary approach for a new student-organized course on the state of the planet's ecological equilibrium. We plan to look at historical aspects of man's use of the environment, at how different cultures have related to the environment and how successful and lasting those relationships have been. We hope to deal with the ethical and aesthetic aspects of environmental deterioration as well as with how past literature may have influenced man's past abuses of nature.

But even without new courses, more than a few words about the environment are already getting around —on the pages of a special, student-published environmental newsletter, which mixes listings of pertinent meetings or hearings with commentary on local and national issues.

Of course, the first thing that anyone who has decided to make a serious and definite commitment to the environmental scene must do is to become well-versed in at least one aspect of the problem. This is not to say we must become restricted specialists. The most effective students at Santa Cruz are generalists. They know how water pollution affects air pollution—and vice versa. They know how agricultural methods affect air pollution, how building methods affect agricultural methods, how mining methods affect water supply. They also know something about the real costs of environmental deterioration. When Governor Ronald Reagan talks about the automobile's impact on the environment, he is talking about very visible problems, like smog, which people can relate to quite readily. But the real costs go far beyond the high price of smog. They include, for example, the cost to the land of strip-mining coal, which is necessary to stoke the furnaces, which are necessary to smelt the steel, which is necessary to produce the automobiles. Steel smelters produce pollution, too. Highways pollute open space. Used car lots pollute cityscapes. Junkyards pollute countrysides. And so it goes.

But most people don't know these things. "We need an education of the heart and spirit," wrote Cedric Wright. "The most important things belong *first,* not last or never."

by Cliff Humphrey

Doing Ecology Action

Ecology Action is what most organizations are not. The four of us who founded it in Berkeley in 1968— Chuck Herrick, Betty Schwimmer, my wife Mary, and I—were "meeting refugees." We wanted to develop a method of facilitating action without the attendant excess baggage of motions, quorums, votes, committees and dues. It seemed to us that soon after a formal, organizational structure was established, especially on a national basis, someone wanted to run it. In the commotion of "wanting to run it," the original purpose of establishing the structure was often trampled underfoot.

We believe that ecology—knowledge of our household—contains an implicit set of ethics for both individual and institutional behavior. Our common physical households—clean air, fresh water, fertile soil—sustains us all in a similar manner. We all share a common culture and economic system that values an increasing amount of health, comfort, joy and security. Yet there are tragic contradictions between these values and our naive attempts to fulfill them. To have knowledge of our household's limitations is to understand these contradictions.

Our planet has a finite amount of arable land. Its diverse processes of air enrichment and fresh water distribution are limited. Its many interdependent forms of

Cliff Humphrey is a recent graduate of the University of California at Berkeley, where he founded Ecology Action.

life all require a very complicated blend of conditions
for a healthy existence. The dominant species, man, also
has serious limitations. He can only deal with a small
amount of information at any one time. This limitation
has resulted in our not knowing the consequences of
our actions.

We have collected in cities and have trusted others
to provide us with food, water, fuel, housing, electricity,
clothing and jobs. Those we have trusted have done
well, according to a limited definition of their "job."
But no one foresaw the eventual results of their labors.
As a consequence, just doing their job has resulted in
the obliteration of arable land, contamination and modification of natural systems, the extinction of many
species, and more than 1½ billion underprivileged
people. All are hungry, but some are dying of starvation
and some have been mentally incapacitated by a hostile
environment.

These contradictions are the specific ingredients of
an abstract event—our extinction. And extinction is
well under way. We are no longer nourishing ourselves
with the clean air, fresh water and nutritious food our
bodies require. Our social environment is preventing us
from realizing our individual potential for joy and
creativity. While there is a remote chance we could
destroy the earth in one final crescendo of booming,
exploding, poisonous hell, it is much more likely that
we will continue to lose our humanness as our vitality,
spirit and strength are insidiously sapped by devices of
our own creation. At what point on such a decline does
man, as defined today, pass into extinction?

Doing ecology action tries to take all of the household's limitations into account and evaluate everything
else in relation to them. Each action large and small is
evaluated simply by asking: does it facilitate our survival? All of our actions are directed at three main
categories of cultural practices:

(1) irrelevant practices—new car models every
year and hard-sell merchandising; (2) necessary

but possibly dangerous practices—food processing and distribution, construction of housing and its organization, the procuring and distribution of energy; (3) destructive practices—social regimentation, covering the soil with concrete, asphalt and buildings, dumping filth into our surroundings, and warfare.

Many environmental groups across the country are focusing on each of the destructive and most of the irrelevant practices. Other groups are watching over the operation of the necessary practices. But the issue of survival transcends all the individual concerns of these groups. For example, if a group brings about a change of practices on a specific issue but, while so doing, contributes to the total destructive impact of many other activities, the end result is a net loss.

Doing ecology action—taking action that follows from knowledge of ecology within the context of our physical and social surroundings—has an intrinsic system of ethics. These ethics are based on one premise: that it is not the purpose or intent of mankind to extinguish life on this planet.

As we enter the 1970's, politically ambitious public servants are already mouthing glaringly irrelevant pronouncements. They are pledging more money to fuel more business to overcome the destructive effects from too much business already. The stock market itself is a glaring contradiction of ecological ethics. A stock's rising price signals our ability to exploit a new portion of our household and the imminence of that exploitation. This means that we have a vested interest in our own destruction.

The groups that call themselves Ecology Action continue to develop ecological ethics and to explore their implications. Some groups feel, from a tactical point of view, that these realities are too harsh for popular consumption. I don't agree. I feel the general public will be relieved to understand that the hectic pace of daily affairs is, in fact, a misguided, destructive endeavor rather than the American Dream. When we relate our actions to the ethics of ecology, basic insecurity will be replaced with a clear vision of what human existence can be.

Specific actions follow from development of the perspective, scope, and ethics of ecology. First, there is education, informing people of the survival crisis. Second, the discovery and clarification of contradictions within our existing activities. Third, the development and implementation of alternatives to the present cultural practices.

Ecology Action groups across the country are engaging in all three activities. Their involvement is not so much the result of any organizing effort as it is a reflection of an emerging awareness of the total consequences of our present cultural practices. Yet some amount of organizational structure is essential. The first level of the structure is individual action, as a private citizen during non-employed time, as an employee of a firm, or as a member of a fraternal organization, citizens' committee or sports club. The second structural level is the group that manifests ecology action. The third is institutional: government, business, educational and legal institutions are all capable of ethically relevant ecology actions. When the combined results of all these actions begin to reclaim our planet's fertility rather than detract from it, we will have developed the optimum organization.

Remember that we are not concerned here merely with the aesthetics of open space, the nice birds, or the reduction of noise in our cities. The issue is survival, for we are fooling with the guts of our entire culture, the lives of at least two hundred million people. Our activities in this cultural area will affect millions of other people in countries from which we are now obtaining our raw materials. We had better know what we are about and take each step with great care. There is not enough time to study our present predicament and then design a total solution, even if it were possible. The parameters of this crisis are changing so quickly that a proper definition cannot be made. Only through intensive universal education and individual actions at all levels of organization can we mount an adequate and flexible response. If we have to wait for an agency to determine policy and implement federal programs, we may be waiting on our own extinction.

Individual action is only limited by an individual's particular situation. For instance, let's follow an imaginary employee of a steel plant through a day of doing ecology action. He will walk, pedal, join a car pool, or ride the bus to work. If he has to drive he will have on his car a sign telling how much air his engine inhales and the nature of its pollution. At work he will post on bulletin boards or available wall space clippings and pictures concerning ecological issues. He will also be on the alert for wasteful corporate methods that should be corrected, and be willing to talk fellow employees into helping him correct a deficiency. If employees are aware of a harmful process that could be corrected, and management refuses to take care of it, the plant should be struck until that practice is corrected. If management wants to clean up but can't afford to pay the price, perhaps some employees will drop by on a Saturday and pitch in.

There is simply no point in thinking about buying survival, because there is not enough money to pay for all the needed action. Each person, group and institution must contribute its own resources. When a natural disaster such as a flood or tornado strikes, we react in this manner. The effectiveness of this response to a natural disaster depends on a cultural consensus that we should respond quickly to alleviate human suffering. But we have no prior experience with survival crises. We have always been able to take life pretty much for granted. We do not, at this time, have a cultural consensus that the issue is one of survival. Education can help bring about this consensus. Demonstrations to point out built-in cultural contradictions can indicate the way to positive alternatives.

In retrospect, our most successful demonstration—

Smog Free Locomotion Day—seems a good balance of education and the revelation of both cultural contradictions and alternatives, in this case, alternatives to the gasoline-powered car. On Saturday, September 27, 1969, we staged a five-mile parade through the streets of Berkeley. Smog-free locomotion was represented by antique steamers, pogo sticks, stilts, electric cars, and bicycles. And we actually buried a Chevrolet V-8 engine under the banner "Bury smog producers before they bury us." We pulled the engine through the streets in a mock coffin.

Some of our earlier actions were an "unfilling" of San Francisco Bay, a tour of the Hayward earthquake fault, and the destruction of our own family automobile. To unfill the bay, we loaded money bags with bay mud and distributed them to the major corporations that have profited from filling the Bay. This project combined education with a clarification of the contradictions between ecological realities and economic expedients. On our Hayward tour, we decorated the fault with purple crepe paper and leaflets describing the dangers of living in this earthquake zone. The Hayward fault is active. It passes through the eastern end of the University of California at Berkeley campus, residence halls, private homes, the California School for the Blind and Deaf, an earth dam, the Bay Area Rapid Transit tunnels, even aqueducts.

At an environmental fair on June 7, 1969, we destroyed our family car, then reconstituted it into a piece of sculpture. I smashed the four-barrel carburetor with a sledge hammer to get things started. In about four hours, sixty people had reduced it to rubble. Now we are planning to convert cars into planter boxes for large trees, "mobile parks" for vacant lots. Just imagine the impact of a twenty-foot tree growing out of a Buick!

Ecology Action groups are proliferating across the country because of the quality of such images.

In Berkeley, the original Ecology Action group has developed a high school text. It is called "What's

Ecology?" and was first used by Bob Evans at Campolindo High School in the Bay area. Now we are revising it for primary and junior high school levels. And as this chapter goes to press, we are completing arrangements for our most ambitious undertaking: a "Survival Walk" from Sacramento to Los Angeles to demonstrate the relationship between the problems of agriculture and of our urban areas.

Unfortunately, there is a growing tendency to find niches or categories for various environmental groups, just as we tend to over-classify environmental problems. The universal nature of the survival crisis transcends all such schemes of classification. An action either relates to survival or it does not. If the ecological movement is going to be effective it must speak to as many people as possible. And the people *will* listen as long as the language they hear is the language of a new age of human maturity.

PART III

---

three activists

"Pessimism has no survival value. Nor hate, nor elitism, nor puritanism."

by Stephanie Mills

. . . O and all the little babies in the Alameda gardens Yes . . .

(Stephanie Mills is a young woman who intends to practice what she preaches. She preaches population control. As valedictorian for the Class of 1969 at Mills College in Oakland, Miss Mills startled her listeners by announcing she does not intend to bring any children into this crowded world. Now 21, Miss Mills continues her personal crusade toward zero-populaton growth as a field representative for Planned Parenthood.)

[1]

I sink I'd die down over his feet, humbly dumbly, only to washup. Yes, tid. There's where. First. We pass through grass behush the the bush to. Whish! A gull. Gulls. Far calls. Coming, far! End here. Us. Then. Finn, again! Take. Bussoftlee, mememormee! Till thousends thee. Lps. The keys to. Given! A way a lone a last a loved a long the

—James Joyce/*Finnegans Wake*

Rivers flow to the sea, clouds rise from the sea, rain falls to the earth and trickles into rivers. All of life moves, if uninterrupted, in cycles. This was Joyce's

77

vision, and must become ours. Life ever-same and ever-changing once was ours. Or ours to lose? Man interrupts cycles, man changes life with no return to same. Man resists death, and by so doing destroys life.

This is where we are now, in this decade. Faced with a final chance to acknowledge the cycle of life and death and flow with it. Faced with the chance to rejoin nature. But faced with the coming of the worst of all possible worlds as well.

The spectacle of the starving child, the sewer/river, the faceless state confronts us now, glaring at us in our corner. Why are we here now? Why must we, of all generations, live in a make-it-or-break-it era? Our world is crowded and poor. Our neighbors are hungry while we waste our food. Our brother animals are dying, and we poisoned them. Ironically, our poisons seem to affect most brutally those creatures who fly, who soar and laugh at us because we cannot fly without clumsy gadgets. We earth-bound humans are only digits now, crowded into anonymity, our lives and individuality diluted by the presence of rapidly doubling billions like us.

Think of how many a billion is for a moment. Can you? Have you ever *seen* a billion things? Can you imagine a billion human beings? Three, or seven billion human beings? The neighborhood will be getting crowded in 2000.

We find ourselves overpopulated because we attempted to thwart death. Western man, through technology, has lengthened his life span by eliminating many diseases. Since the beginning of this century, missionaries of public health have brought to most of the underdeveloped nations of the world the techniques of achieving longer life. The application of these techniques, by thwarting death temporarily, upset the balance between birth rates and death rates. The growth rates of populations skyrocketed: more human beings lived long enough to produce more children, who had a better chance to survive. Etcetera. Ad infinitum.

[II]

What does it matter? What I hate is death and disease, as you well know. And whether you wish it or not, we're allies, facing them and fighting them together.
—Albert Camus/*The Plague*

These words are uttered by a doctor at the height of an outbreak of bubonic plague. Dr. Rieux has long since recognized that the plague will run its course, in spite of his efforts to combat the disease. Rieux, nonetheless, is dignified by his resistance to the inevitable.

Nobody can deny that the elimination of disease is desirable. There is a case to be made, however, against upsetting a natural balance. For balance, isn't it conceivable that birth control *could* have been employed simultaneously with death control? This is the advantage of hindsight. Yet vigorous population control is still not considered a complementary health measure—and we sink deeper into the morass of too many every day.

Birth control is regarded as tampering with nature. Death control is not. Those people who denounce contraception as interference with a Supreme Will do not, by the same token, denounce typhoid shots. For birth control is regarded as political, not medical. Swallowing Enovid is certainly more emotionally-charged than popping tetracycline. But both actions involve tinkering with the natural order of things.

Acceptance of birth control is absolutely necessary for a humane solution to the population crisis. And it *is* a technical solution. The alternative "natural" solution is to eliminate death control.

There is this to be said of population at this time: the birth rates must go down or the death rates will soon go up. By the Eighties, widespread and cataclysmic death may be caused by hunger, plague, war, or environmental disaster.

Death is finiteness, and Western man rejects finiteness. We long for a limitless supply of everything: air, water, food, wilderness, time, and frontier. But our infinity is linear. We head in a straight, unswerving line for the cosmos, damning any obstacle—even scientific fact—that stands in the way. Sadly enough, as we strive for infinity, we create the irreversible limits. To acquire more electricity and more water, we dam and destroy Glen Canyon for all time. To acquire more food, we deprive the pelican of his—and destroy it, too. For all time. The roster of deaths we have caused in our rush for life is almost endless. And as more of us come into being, *more* death.

More people, we believe, means more power, more consumers, more GNP. Score three. But more people are less individual. More people are less free. A more populous nation becomes necessarily more authoritarian. And beneath the veneer roils a cesspool of chaos.

[III]

> Listen! If all must suffer to pay for the eternal harmony, what have children to do with it, tell me please? It's beyond all comprehension why they should suffer, and why they should pay for the harmony.
> —Feodor Dostoevski/*The Brothers Karamazov*

Children are the first to die of hunger, children are rebirth, and children are what the concern with population is all about. Children of all ages are the solution.

Population growth intensifies the spate of problems which confront the earth today. Ignoring the population crisis precludes solving the problems of war, hunger, disease, and alienation. Numbers *per se* cause none of these, but mega-behavior and mega-societies will be fraught with all of them. Curiously enough, a recognition of the population problem and its solution—population control—is avoided by all those who have the power to effect the change.

It took a child to perceive the Emperor's nudity, since all the *loyal* subjects had their perceptions filtered politically.

Our emperors would parade their new clothes of environment, simply by announcing that the problems of environment and population will be solved. Thus far, the clothes are invisible, for meaningful solutions to the population-environment crisis must be drastic indeed. They require a revolution in consciousness.

Solving the population problem will require a reorientation of child-bearing attitudes. To encourage such a reorientation, alternative satisfactions must be provided. New modalities of family living such as communes and kibbutzes might be tried. Certainly women's roles must be expanded to encompass much, much more than the production of children. A cultural inversion must take place. The "old maid," not the mother of twelve, must be made the heroine. The childless couple should be applauded, not pitied. And the adopted baby should become the "real" baby (as he always has been).

A danger inherent in the population problem is that the state may finally assume control of reproduction if the individual doesn't. Consider a state so powerful that it controls the reproduction of its citizens. Consider, also, a nation so overpopulated that it can't survive unless drastic steps are taken to alleviate the whole complex of environmental problems.

The opportunity to assume individual responsibility is still ours, but not, perhaps, for long. If individuals abdicate this responsibility, if individuals refuse to act in their enlightened self-interest, then the state will surely take a hand in individual affairs, sooner than later.

Perhaps there is an element of self-fulfilling prophecy in such a warning. Perhaps such fears should not be voiced. Perhaps. Yet we must realize our role in the continuum of evolution. And such realization may lead us to some interesting questions. Is it our turn to become extinct as a species? Is there any point in undertaking a serious attempt to survive? Is there any wisdom in challenging what would seem the inevitable?

These questions are unanswerable; yet the image of

Dr. Rieux, fighting impersonal annihilation, is inspiring. Resisting death is humane. But the death we must resist is more than the death of mankind. It is the death of the ecosystem.

[IV]

In gloomy times of bloody confusion
Ordered disorder
Planful wilfulness
Dehumanized humanity
When there is no end to the unrest in our cities:
In such a world, a world like a slaughter-house—
Summoned by rumors of threatening deeds of violence
To prevent the brute strength of the short-sighted people
From shattering its own tools and
Trampling its own bread-basket to pieces—
We wish to reintroduce
God.
  —Bertold Brecht/*Saint Joan of the Stockyards*

Not a bad idea. It all depends, however, on which god is reintroduced. Will it be the anthropocentric god of Genesis, or a dryad? Or can this god/godliness be so personal, so innate, that it has no name?

It's not enough to survive, hard as that alone may be. It may not be worth it to survive in a world devoid of humane beings, a world in which man's only aspiration is for biological existence. Quality of life is the concern, and life has no quality without some experience of god. The experience may not even be describable. Can you describe the wisdom of the ecosystem, the flash of awareness that comes when you perceive how the planet functions? Every organism relates to every other. God is an inadequate word.

Man's aspirations so far have been guided by the god of Genesis. For the most part, we have been proud of our subjugation of the planet. Now we are finding that our aspirations have been misguided and destructive. Where can humanity direct its aspirations, now that we see the futility of damming, grading, eroding, over-breeding?

To aspire to survival and to aspire to humanity are the paths. They are one and the same. For openers, we can turn to the humanity within us, and must to survive. All the logic, precision, and practicality in the world can't save us if we lose our own souls.

The prescription is nothing less than a revolution in consciousness. We are beginning to see it now, and must participate. It takes more than lockjawed resolution to save a world for all creatures. It takes love and joy. There can be no survival without passion. Passion for humanity, love of the earth, joy of existence, and hope for the future. A very wise man has said that "Pessimism has no survival value." Nor hate, nor elitism, nor puritanism.

> *. . . O and the sea the sea crimson sometimes like fire and the glorious sunsets and the fig-trees in the Alameda gardens Yes and all the queer little streets and pink and blue and yellow houses and the rosegardens and the jessamine and geraniums and cactuses and Gibraltar as a girl where I was a Flower of the mountain yes when I put the rose in my hair like the Andalusian girls used or shall I wear red yes and how he kissed me under the Moorish wall and I thought well as well him as another and then I asked him with my eyes to ask again yes and then he asked me would I yes to say yes my mountain flower and first I put my arms around him yes and drew him down to me so he could feel my breasts all perfume yes and his heart was going like mad and yes I said yes I will Yes.*

> —Joyce, again/*Ulysses*

by Pat Smith and Mariana Gosnell

That Snyder Sutra

Most critics and anthologists place naturalist-poet Gary
Snyder among the Beats, that generation of bust-out
writers that searched through the early Fifties for a
battleground on which they, like their predecessors,
could shed their literary blood. But with World War II
and Korea having arrived a bit too early and Viet Nam
a little too late, the Beats—who had been nurtured on
the robust exotica of Hemingway, Steinbeck, Dos Passos
and Thomas Wolfe—retreated into the cities (New
York, San Francisco and Mexico City, mainly), where
they sucked on marijuana and talked about each other.
Occasionally, they wrote.

A few of them found their way out. Following the
lead of their chronicler, Jack Kerouac, a handful of
Beats left the cities and moved up into the great green
promise of Big Sur. Amid this new world, their minds
were refreshed and their literature suddenly shifted
from the anguished cries of the restless to the sweet
cogent songs of the reborn. No longer did they thirst for
battle. Realizing how clean, peaceful and ordered the
world was made to be, they saw the wilderness not as
the Last Frontier of Hemingway and Dos Passos, but
as the last resort of modern man. No longer were deer,
bear and birds objects to be hunted, nor trees giants to
be felled, nor rivers and streams toilets for industrial

Pat Smith, a former outdoors columnist, is now an associate editor,
and Mariana Gosnell an assistant editor, with *Newsweek* magazine.

and human wastes. Suddenly, the collective voice of the Beats joined other voices crying from the wilderness. It was a chorus calculated to electrify the young.

Now 40-years-young, Snyder stands at the cutting edge of the eco-activist movement. It is, perhaps, a strange place for so gentle a man to be. Though he has participated in a lion's share of demonstrative activities (he is active in both Ecology Action and Friends of the Earth), his most effective contribution to the cause has been as a lecturer and writer who campaigns through his poetry (he has published six volumes). "I attack on the level of archetypes, myth, symbol, image to help push the minds of young people," says Snyder. "I make nature not an enemy but a great goddess, something not to be afraid of but to consider a true home." And the young listen. At one recent reading, 3,000 people showed up to hear Snyder and several other poets hold forth "for the benefit of ecology."

No one is more qualified to benefit ecology. Snyder grew up in the woods of Washington State where, at an early age, he developed a mystical rapport with nature. "I had a perception as a child," he recalls, "of the destructiveness of the machine. I saw the woods being raped." So Snyder took up the study of nature in earnest and soon discovered something about his fellow man as well: the local residents, mostly farmers, were largely ignorant about the land that fed them. "They knew nothing about the woods," he says. "They had none of the Indian finesse."

What the white man couldn't teach him, Snyder discovered from the American Indian. At Reed College, he specialized in the history and culture of the Indians of the Northwest and set up his bed in a communal house—"like the Hippies did 15 years later." During summer vacations, he returned to the woods to work as a logger or fire-fighter, or to backpack into the deeper wilderness. Some communion with wilderness, according to Snyder, is ultimately necessary for every human. "The wild is in our blood," he says. "And what supports us is, in effect, a wild system. An encounter with

the wild allows our instincts and drives to flow freely
out of ourselves, and it allows us to be in touch with
the wilderness in ourselves." Of those who fear the
woods, the wildness, Snyder is suspicious. He views
them all as its potential rapists. But a man who looks
nature in the eye squarely is unafraid of death, the poet
observes in his environmental manifesto *Four Changes*.
His desire for artificial stability is diminished "because
he can accept his place in a process far greater than
himself."

This notion of man and his inner wilderness devel-
oped into a personal philosophy when Snyder studied
the teachings of Zen during a nine-year stay in Japan.
Basically turned off as a child by what he calls the
"Old Testament's injunction to conquer the landscape,"
Snyder found the Buddhist words closer to the mark:
"Not only men but animals, not only animals but grasses
and stones are capable of winning enlightenment."

Now residing in Mill Valley, north of San Francisco,
Snyder is quite clearly the sum of his experience.
With his Japanese wife, Masa (whom he married on the
rim of an active volcano), and his two sons Kai and
Gen, he divides his days writing poetry and watching
four deer that feed regularly in the back yard. And he
plans to build a house soon in the hills for a "small
community of close friends." But Snyder vows that it
won't be a retreat. He plans to take in dropouts and
ghetto children for two-week stays. "We hope," he says,
"that black kids will learn that they have a stake in
America that lies far beyond the ghetto, the suburbs and
even the farms. That's all white country." Rather, he
sees the black man's turf extending to the public lands
that sprawl over three-quarters of the Western U.S.

Snyder has come to be identified with the concept
of communes, and he regards them not as cop-outs but
as places where one can learn to live simply, close to
the earth, and in small cooperative bands. "Communes
are taking the major problems of our society head-on,"
he says. "They're searching for a way back to our

place in nature." And he points out that communes are not being established on prime soil, but on the marginal land that has been left behind as battered evidence of the great industrial stampede of the 20th Century. In addition, Snyder sees the commune as futuristic. "The kids are making the land productive and green again," he explains. "Someone must get to know the land up close." When the teeth of industry finally wear down —or break off—Snyder's communal children will know how to go on living.

Communes may be essential to an ecological realignment in yet another, more fundamental sense. As Snyder sees it, "You just can't say, 'Stop air pollution with a better stack filter.' The problem has got to be attacked through our culture." The present thrust of technology, he adds, is at odds with the extraordinarily complex structure of nature. "Ecology demonstrates on the empirical level the myriad interrelationships in nature. Buddhism, on another level, asserts the same interdependence of each of the elements."

Snyder maintains there are three societies in America running together: Black, hippie and "mainline state culture." The ideas and impulses underlying the hippie subculture have been around forever, he says, but "it's interesting that they assert themselves now." The contrast between the hippies and the mainliners could be drawn in terms of the spiritual versus the materialistic. And while the back-to-nature movement will effect deep changes in the reigning culture, it will not, according to Snyder, emerge as the dominant force. So be it. Yet the movement will have been a success if everyman—at least once some day—feels a measure of the love Snyder felt when he wrote in his volume, *Back Country:*

> . . . *In this burning, muddy, lying,*
> *blood-drenched world*
> *that quiet meeting in the mountains*
> *cool and gentle as the muzzles of*
> *three elk, helps keep me sane.*

by Constance L. Stallings

It's June in December

A frosty day in Manhattan-Town: bundled up against the 12 degree cold, a dozen young people are picketing the General Motors Building on Fifth Avenue. Around their necks hang oversize black-and-white photographs of exhaust billowing from automobile tailpipes, and aerial views of smog-laden cities. In their hands are flyers that ask a harsh question: "Is General Motors Killing You?" The flyers also quote the Congressional Record of December 16, 1969: "General Motors is responsible for one-third of the polluted air in the country . . . The automotive industry itself accounts for more than 60 percent. In cities, this figure often rises to 85 percent. In New York City, deaths from respiratory diseases have risen more than 700 percent in the last 15 years."

One brown-haired girl stands out among the pickets. She is dressed in almost-knee-high boots, a yellow mini showing a scant two inches below her pea jacket, a striped wool scarf knotted fetchingly under her chin. She approaches each passerby with a sweet smile, and says: "Sir, General Motors is killing us." She thrusts a flyer into a gentleman's hand. And he says, "You'd better believe it, sister!"—and walks away, reading.

The girl: "Hi, GM is endangering your life." A guy.

Constance L. Stallings, assistant editor of this handbook, is a former editor and photographer for *Open Space Action* magazine.

"I own a Volkswagen." The girl (laughing): "Well, that's a *little* better."

Again, the girl: "Ma'am, 25 percent more lung cancer." Fur-coated matron: "That's right. Absolutely true."

And the truth of the whole business was that the earnest young girl and her friends from *Environment!* seemed as welcome to the ladies and businessmen of upper Fifth Avenue as a warm breeze from the South. It was like, well, June in December. No one was nasty. No one accused them of being revolutionaries. Nobody dropped a single handout to the sidewalk during the entire demonstration. Even the attendant cop went out of his way to be helpful to the pickets. Despite the cold, strangers took the time to offer their congratulations, and went away in apparent agreement that General Motors had, indeed, no right to be murdering the air.

But who is the girl in the yellow mini? Who is the *girl?* It's December Duke, at 19, already a total environment activist.

The action started last spring in Miami, December's home town, when she was hired by scientist Luther Gerlock to interview young people to determine their degree of environmental awareness. "What I found out," says December, "was that they didn't have much, so I decided to create it." With Philip Spitzer, 21, December organized a group of about 40 young people just out of high school, and appropriated for themselves the name *Environment!* For advice, December wrote to Wes Fischer, head of the University of Minnesota's Students for Environmental Defense. "I rapped to him about our problems. Wes's group had been active for quite a while. I asked him about their tactics. They turned out to be pretty dramatic." *Environment!* decided to be dramatic, too.

"First off, we did an embarrassing thing," December recalls. "We walked up and down the Key Biscayne beaches, looking for people who littered. Then we'd go up and talk to them. Our main thing was to explain how uneconomical it was—the economic stupidity of making a mess." On the whole, the litterers were embarrassed, and apologetic. That was last May. Since then, other *Environment!* activists have been continuing the beach patrols every other week, and conditions have improved. (Lifeguards, in fact, have begun to hand out dollar litter tickets.)

In town, *Environment!* volunteers started prowling Miami's main streets, watching for women in animal-skin coats. Says December: "We'd go up to a woman and say, 'Did you know that five leopards were butchered for your back?' But if you want to know the truth, those women were real bitches about it. They'd say, 'The animals are dead, aren't they?' or try to make us believe their coats were made of fake fur."

Undaunted, December branched out in new directions.

There was, for example, the Peanut Shell caper. To demonstrate the ineffectiveness of the city's sewerage treatment system, which drains into Biscayne Bay, she hit on the ingenious tactic of flushing peanut shells down the toilets of Miami's City Hall. Then: "We all went down to the Bay to see the shells bobbing around." Though the caper's findings were duly reported, Miami is yet to improve its waste disposal procedures.

And the business at Turkey Point. South Florida conservationists had been making noises about thermal pollution caused by the Turkey Point nuclear power plant, 20 miles south of Miami. But would the plant operators admit it? Of course not. They insisted they were only making good electricity. But December had another ingenious idea. She called up all the people she could think of, and invited them to go skin-diving on weekends, right in front of the Turkey Point plant, to measure the damage for themselves. One measurement: "The water's so hot you get a headache after 10 minutes." Turkey Point is still operating, but at least its thermal pollution has been dramatized in human terms.

Helping to save the Everglades was probably Miami *Environment!*'s greatest success. Last spring, Joe

Browder, the National Audubon Society's representative for the Southeast U.S., took December to the Big Cypress Swamp and explained the damage a proposed jetport there would visit on the ecology of Everglades National Park. December moved fast. She wangled permission from the Dade County Commissioners for groups to visit the jetport site, under the guise of archaeological exploration. (As it turned out, 40-foot-deep pits gouged out during the construction of the training strip had indeed exposed some interesting fossils.) December organized caravans of high school and university students, led them to the Big Cypress each weekend, then publicized the expeditions by putting up posters all over Miami. "We'd walk around the swamp for a couple of hours, talking, explaining," says December. "We didn't tell people to come out against the jetport. We only said, 'The jetport will have these consequences.' "

As of January, 1970, some *Environment!* members were still conducting tours through the swamp, while others spoke at local schools, spreading the word about the Everglades ecology. The Miami group now functions out of a little red shack owned by the University of Miami botany department.

"Florida's ecology is changing faster than any place in the country," December declares. "The problems there are critical. Environmental groups are starting up all over the state, and in other places in the South, too." Who are they? "I predicted there would be mostly radicals in the environment activist movement, but I found out differently. Even the John Birchers are getting into it. You can get anybody involved when you hit him on his own ground."

Still, it is difficult to explain December's commitment. You ask her about it and she is genuinely puzzled. "Well," she asks. "What committed the *other* activists?" (Never mind that most of them are graduate students.) Before her Miami involvement, December had had no previous activist experience. She lived with her mother— "*Culturally* active, but that's all." True, her sister was involved in the Columbia University sit-in, and now runs a resister's coffeehouse near Fort Dix. But how do you explain the sister? Why aren't both of them lying about on the beaches, slathering on the suntan lotion and combing the sand out of their hair? "Well," December giggles defensively, "I do that *some* of the time."

December attended school in Florida until her high school graduation last year. Since September, 1969, she's been living in New York City where she attends the Katharine Gibbs Secretarial School. "I want to learn all about big business and industry, and the mind of the polluter," she explains. "I need to know their ways. Knowing, maybe I can change them a little. Have you ever thought what would happen if there were a nation-wide secretarial strike?"

Late in the fall of '69, December and a friend, Tom Stokes, organized the New York *Environment!* group. It now has an office at 119 Fifth Avenue. Stokes raised the necessary money from friends—no foundation help. "We don't play with foundations," says December. "They represent the polluters."

Environment!'s aim is participatory ecology. For starters, to call public attention to endangered species, December and Bonnie Green one day dressed themselves up like alligators (in papier-mâché) and paraded back and forth in front of the New York City Gucci store, which was then selling items made from alligator hides. Their costumes drew frisky comments ("Do you bite?")—and lots of newspaper coverage. Later, December and Bonnie were among the 40 participants from several conservation groups demonstrating outside Ben Kahn's, the furrier. Placards! "Did you know that *60,000 cats* are imported illegally every year?" Success! After the pickets left, Kahn signed a pledge not to import the skins of endangered animal species. *Environment!* now has similar participatory activities planned for every weekend.

They're trying to arrange a Bike Day during which a large group of cyclists will pedal around the Wall Street district, protesting the internal combustion engine. "Say, wouldn't you like to see a car-less street in Manhattan?" December asks. "Wow. Trees, and benches, and people sitting around, and no exhaust."

They're involved in researching methods to recycle waste: "We don't want people to think of waste as *waste,* but as something that may be useful in another form."

They want to start training citizens to make pollution complaints.

They'd like to start picketing supermarkets that sell non-biodegradable detergents. December believes that the housewife is going to have to change if the world is going to change for the better: "She ought to be returning bottles, but she's lazy. If we hit the supermarkets, we might have an effect."

They're arranging for a young people's trip to Machiasport, Maine, where the coastline has been threatened by oil refineries. Barbara Hults, the expedition leader, emphasizes: "We're going there to learn, not to tell people what to do." And December says: "We need to check out our facts."

December's typical day involves school from 9 A.M. to 3:30 P.M., then an afternoon working for *Environment!* "Mostly I'm out circulating. I go to S.I.P.I. (Scientists' Institute for Public Information) and copy their material for our research. Sometimes I speak to groups, like Citizens for a Quieter City. I meet people, talk to people. I believe in participatory ecology." Weekends, when she isn't demonstrating, December might be guiding her nine-year-old brother through a Long Island wildlife sanctuary. After one recent expedition, brother went home and promptly gave his mother a hard time for owning a leopard-skin coat. "Children can absorb a lot more than they're given credit for," says December. "If we can hit the young kids and the high school students, we've got it made."

December hasn't forgotten her home state. It seems that several Miami beaches have been closed to bathers (only sunning allowed) because of the danger of typhoid from polluted water. So December has prepared a leaflet for distribution at airports throughout the U.S. It reads: "Don't Go to Florida without Your Typhoid Shot."

December's dream is to lead caravans of activists around the country, meeting local people, rapping, learning local environmental problems—"not to *solve* the problems, but to help get things started. Nobody really knows what to do yet about anything much, but some of our methods *have* been effective. So we have to get together with each other. It beats reading pamphlets." No argument.

PART IV

the land

"We may be perfectly sure of where we are in relation to the supermarket and the next coffee break, but I doubt that any of us knows where he is in relation to the stars and the solstices."

by N. Scott Momaday

An American Land Ethic

One night a strange thing happened. I had written the greater part of *The Way to Rainy Mountain*—all of it, in fact, except the epilogue. I had set down the last of the old Kiowa tales, and I had composed both the historical and the autobiographical commentaries for it. I had the sense of being out of breath, of having said what it was in me to say on that subject. The manuscript lay before me in the bright light, small, to be sure, but complete; or nearly so. I had written the second of the two poems in which that book is framed. I had uttered the last word, as it were. And yet a whole, penultimate piece was missing. I began once again to write:

During the first hours after midnight on the morning of November 13, 1833, it seemed that the world was coming to an end. Suddenly the stillness of the night was broken; there were brilliant flashes of light in the sky, light of such intensity that people were awakened by it. With the speed and density of a driving rain, stars were falling in

N. Scott Momaday, whose first novel, *House Made of Dawn,* was awarded the 1969 Pulitzer Prize for fiction, is a Kiowa Indian and associate professor of English and Comparative Literature at the University of California at Berkeley.

the universe. Some were brighter than Venus; one
was said to be as large as the moon.

I went on to say that that event, the falling of the stars
on North America, that explosion of Leonid meteors
which occurred 137 years ago, is among the earliest
entries in the Kiowa calendars. So deeply impressed
upon the imagination of the Kiowas is that old
phenomenon that it is remembered still; it has become
a part of the racial memory.

"The living memory," I wrote, "and the verbal tradi-
tion which transcends it, were brought together for me
once and for all in the person of Ko-sahn." It seemed
eminently right for me to deal, after all, with that old
woman. Ko-sahn is among the most venerable people
I have ever known. She spoke and sang to me one
summer afternoon in Oklahoma. It was like a dream.
When I was born she was already old; she was a grown
woman when my grandparents came into the world. She
sat perfectly still, folded over on herself. It did not seem
possible that so many years—a century of years—could
be so compacted and distilled. Her voice shuddered, but
it did not fail. Her songs were sad. An old whimsy, a
delight in language and in remembrance, shone in her
one good eye. She conjured up the past, imagining perfectly the long continuity of her being. She imagined the
lovely young girl, wild and vital, she had been. She
imagined the Sun Dance:

There was an old, old woman. She had something
on her back. The boys went out to see. The old
woman had a bag full of earth on her back. It was
a certain kind of sandy earth. That is what they
must have in the lodge. The dancers must dance
upon the sandy earth. The old woman held a dig-
ging tool in her hand. She turned towards the south
and pointed with her lips. It was like a kiss, and
she began to sing:

We have brought the earth.
Now it is time to play;
As old as I am, I still have the feeling of play.

That was the beginning of the Sun Dance.

By this time I was back into the book, caught up completely in the act of writing. I had projected myself—imagined myself—out of the room and out of time. I was there with Ko-sahn in the Oklahoma July. We laughed easily together; I felt that I had known her all of my life—all of hers. I did not want to let her go. But I had come to the end. I set down, almost grudgingly, the last sentences:

It was—all of this and more—a quest, a going forth upon the way to Rainy Mountain. Probably Ko-sahn too is dead now. At times, in the quiet of evening, I think she must have wondered, dreaming, who she was. Was she become in her sleep that old purveyor of the sacred earth, perhaps, that ancient one who, old as she was, still had the feeling of play? And in her mind, at times, did she see the falling stars?

For some time I sat looking down at these words on the page, trying to deal with the emptiness that had come about inside of me. The words did not seem real. The longer I looked at them, the more unfamiliar they became. At last I could scarcely believe that they made sense, that they had anything whatsoever to do with meaning. In desperation almost, I went back over the final paragraphs, backwards and forwards, hurriedly. My eyes fell upon the name Ko-sahn. And all at once everything seemed suddenly to refer to that name. The name seemed to humanize the whole complexity of language. All at once, absolutely, I had the sense of the magic of words and of names. Ko-sahn, I said. And I said again KO-SAHN.

Then it was that that ancient, one-eyed woman

Ko-sahn stepped out of the language and stood before
me on the page. I was amazed, of course, and yet it
seemed to me entirely appropriate that this should
happen.

"Yes, grandson," she said. "What is it? What do you
want?"

"I was just now writing about you," I replied, stam-
mering. "I thought—forgive me—I thought that perhaps
you were . . . that you had . . ."

"No," she said. And she cackled, I thought. And she
went on. "You have imagined me well, and so I am.
You have imagined that I dream, and so I do. I have
seen the falling stars."

"But all of this, this *imagining*," I protested, "this
has taken place—is taking place in my mind. You are
not actually here, not here in this room." It occurred to
me that I was being extremely rude, but I could not help
myself. She seemed to understand.

"Be careful of your pronouncements, grandson," she
answered. "You imagine that I am here in this room, do
you not? That is worth something. You see, I have
existence, whole being, in your imagination. It is but
one kind of being, to be sure, but it is perhaps the best
of all kinds. If I am not here in this room, grandson,
then surely neither are you."

"I think I see what you mean," I said. I felt justly
rebuked. "Tell me, grandmother, how old are you?"

"I do not know," she replied. "There are times when
I think that I am the oldest woman on earth. You know,
the Kiowas came into the world through a hollow log.
In my mind's eye I have seen them emerge, one by one,
from the mouth of the log. I have seen them so clearly,
how they were dressed, how delighted they were to see
the world around them. I *must* have been there. And
I must have taken part in that old migration of the
Kiowas from the Yellowstone to the Southern Plains,
for I have seen antelope bounding in the tall grass near
the Big Horn River, and I have seen the ghost forests in
the Black Hills. Once I saw the red cliffs of Palo Duro

Canyon. I was with those who were camped in the Wichita Mountains when the stars fell."

"You are indeed very old," I said, "and you have seen many things."

"Yes, I imagine that I have," she replied. Then she turned slowly around, nodding once, and receded into the language I had made. And then I imagined I was alone in the room.

[II]

Once in his life a man ought to concentrate his mind upon the remembered earth, I believe. He ought to give himself up to a particular landscape in his experience, to look at it from as many angles as he can, to wonder about it, to dwell upon it. He ought to imagine that he touches it with his hands at every season and listens to the sounds that are made upon it. He ought to imagine the creatures there and all the faintest motions of the wind. He ought to recollect the glare of noon and all the colors of the dawn and dusk.

The Wichita Mountains rise out of the Southern Plains in a long crooked line that runs from east to west. The mountains are made of red earth, and of rock that is neither red nor blue but some very rare admixture of the two, like the feathers of certain birds. They are not so high and mighty as the mountains of the Far West, and they bear a different relationship to the land around them. One does not imagine that they are distinctive in themselves, or indeed that they exist apart from the plain in any sense. If you try to think of them in the abstract, they lose the look of mountains. They are preeminently an expression of the larger landscape, more perfectly organic than one can easily imagine. To behold these mountains from the plain is one thing; to see the plain from the mountains is something else. I have stood on the top of Mt. Scott and seen the earth below, bending out into the whole circle of the sky. The wind runs always close upon the slopes, and there are times when you can hear the rush of it like water in the ravines.

Here is the hub of an old commerce. A hundred years ago the Kiowas and Comanches journeyed outward from the Wichitas in every direction, seeking after mischief and medicine, horses and hostages. Sometimes they went away for years, but they always returned, for the land had got hold of them. It is a consecrated place, and even now there is something of the wilderness about it. There is a game preserve in the hills. Animals graze away in the open meadows or, closer by, keep to the shadows of the groves: antelope and deer, longhorns and buffalo. It was here, the Kiowas say, that the first buffalo came into the world.

The yellow, grassy knoll that is called Rainy Mountain lies a short distance to the north and west. There, on the west side, is the ruin of an old school where my grandmother went as a wild young girl in blanket and braids to learn of numbers and of names in English. And there she is buried.

Most is your name the name of this dark stone.
Deranged in death, the mind to be inheres
Forever in the nominal unknown,
The wake of nothing audible he hears
Who listens here and now to hear your name.

The early sun, red as a hunter's moon,
Runs in the plain. The mountain burns and shines;
And silence is the long approach of noon
Upon the shadow that your name defines—
And death this cold, black density of stone.

[III]

I am interested in the way that a man looks at a given landscape and takes possession of it in his blood and brain. For this happens, I am certain, in the ordinary

motion of life. None of us lives apart from the land
entirely; such an isolation is unimaginable. We have
sooner or later to come to terms with the world around
us—and I mean especially the physical world, not only
as it is revealed to us immediately through our senses,
but also as it is perceived more truly in the long turn of
seasons and of years. And we must come to moral
terms. There is no alternative, I believe, if we are to
realize and maintain our humanity, for our humanity
must consist in part in the ethical as well as the practical
ideal of preservation. And particularly here and now is
that true. We Americans need now more than ever before—and indeed more than we know—to imagine who
and what we are with respect to the earth and sky. I am
talking about an act of the imagination essentially, and
the concept of an American land ethic.

It is no doubt more difficult to imagine in 1970 the
landscape of America than it was in, say, 1900. Our
whole experience as a nation in this century has been a
repudiation of the pastoral ideal which informs so much
of the art and literature of the nineteenth century. One
effect of the Technological Revolution has been to
uproot us from the soil. We have become disoriented, I
believe; we have suffered a kind of psychic dislocation
of ourselves in time and space. We may be perfectly sure
of where we are in relation to the supermarket and the
next coffee break, but I doubt that any of us knows
where he is in relation to the stars and to the solstices.
Our sense of the natural order has become dull and un-
reliable. Like the wilderness itself, our sphere of instinct
has diminished in proportion as we have failed to
imagine truly what it is. And yet I believe that it is
possible to formulate an ethical idea of the land—a
notion of what it is and must be in our daily lives—and
I believe moreover that it is absolutely necessary to do
so.

It would seem on the surface of things that a land
ethic is something that is alien to, or at least dormant in,
most Americans. Most of us in general have developed

an attitude of indifference toward the land. In terms of my own experience, it is difficult to see how such an attitude could ever have come about.

[IV]

Ko-sahn could remember where my grandmother was born. "It was just there," she said, pointing to a tree, and the tree was like a hundred others that grew up in the broad depression of the Washita River. I could see nothing to indicate that anyone had ever been there, spoken so much as a word, or touched the tips of his fingers to the tree. But in her memory Ko-sahn could see the child. I think she must have remembered my grandmother's voice, for she seemed for a long moment to listen and to hear. There was a still, heavy heat upon that place; I had the sense that ghosts were gathering there.

And in the racial memory, Ko-sahn had seen the falling stars. For her there was no distinction between the individual and the racial experience, even as there was none between the mythical and the historical. Both were realized for her in the one memory, and that was of the land. This landscape, in which she had lived for a hundred years, was the common denominator of everything that she knew and would ever know—and her knowledge was profound. Her roots ran deep into the earth, and from those depths she drew strength enough to hold still against all the forces of chance and disorder. And she drew therefrom the sustenance of meaning and of mystery as well. The falling stars were not for Ko-sahn an isolated or accidental phenomenon. She had a great personal investment in that awful commotion of light in the night sky. For it remained to be imagined. She must at last deal with it in words; she must appropriate it to her understanding of the whole universe. And, again, when she spoke of the Sun Dance, it was an essential expression of her relationship to the life of the earth and to the sun and moon.

In Ko-sahn and in her people we have always had

the example of a deep, ethical regard for the land. We had better learn from it. Surely that ethic is merely latent in ourselves. It must now be activated, I believe. We Americans must come again to a moral comprehension of the earth and air. We must live according to the principle of a land ethic. The alternative is that we shall not live at all.

by Robert Michael Pyle

Union Bay: A Life-after-death Plant-in

Union Bay is a tiny appendage of Lake Washington, on
Seattle's east side. A half-century ago, when canals and
locks were constructed to join Union Bay with Lake
Union and that lake with salt-water Puget Sound, the
water level of the bay fell and vast marshes emerged
along its gently sloping shores. In time, these marshes
evolved into one of the finest wildlife habitats in western
Washington. The diversity and abundance of life forms
in the area soon inspired a book, *Union Bay: The Life
of a City Marsh,* by Seattle naturalists Harry Higman
and Earl Larrison. When the book was published in
1951 more than 125 species of birds could be found
there, as well as substantial populations of weasel, mink,
beaver, muskrat, and otter.

For a time, Union Bay remained undisturbed. To the
east opened the broad, uncluttered expanse of Lake
Washington, and beyond the Seattle skyline rose the in-
comparable Cascades. The northern shores attracted
residential neighborhoods of pleasing quality. On the
west: the largest and most renowned educational institution in the region, the University of Washington. Beyond the academic buildings, the Montlake Ship Canal
merged the waters of the two Unions, its high sides
draped with ivy and studded with holly and birches. And

Robert Michael Pyle is a 22-year-old free-lance writer and graduate
student in the University of Washington's College of Forest Resources.

above the gothic, copper-cupola towers of the Montlake Bridge, beyond the yachts and houseboats of Lake Union, rose the profile of the magnificent Olympic Mountains on their distant peninsula. Finally, to the south, on a fogless day, Mt. Rainier dominated the horizon.

When I came to the university as a student in 1965, I was immediately attracted to the marsh below the campus. Crossing an enormous parking lot which had been implanted beside the bay, I sometimes paused to watch the mallards or the mountains. Occasionally, I also canoed along the watercourses of the university arboretum, passing in and out of stark pillars which supported a freeway approach to the new, concrete Evergreen Point Floating Bridge. I was less surprised by the pillars than by what seemed to be a surfeit of nature remaining in a modern city of more than half a million people.

As my appreciation for the whole of the natural and wild scene deepened, I began to wonder what the bay might have been like before the freeway. And I found part of the answer in the book *Union Bay*. Now, I walked and paddled in the same places as before, but with different eyes. Now the swampy edges of the bay shrank into their proper perspective: Mere fragments they were, tattered and incomplete, barely reminiscent of the great refuge of the previous decade. Now the freeway in the arboretum zoomed into sharp focus. This road was not a positive thing which, by the beneficence of its engineers, had preserved something of the green scene; rather it was a callous intrusion, a preposterous travesty which subverted totally the purposes of the arboretum. Looking for once beyond the small, reedy islands and the sparsely grown shoreline, I realized that the monolithic blight of the Montlake Dump had once been marsh. It had taken three years and a telling book, but now I recognized Union Bay for what it was: Not a fortuitous condition of values preserved but rather a condition of heinous disturbance, where some small vestige of the natural ecology still struggled to maintain its integrity.

How could the university have allowed this to happen? Perhaps government pressures to route the freeway through the arboretum had been too great to combat in those days of an unaroused public. Still, the sanitary fill which had supplanted so viciously the superb north marsh had been sanctioned, even encouraged, by the university. While many colleges spend large sums to acquire accessible study areas where biological instruction and investigation can be carried out in the field, the University of Washington already had an ecological wonderland literally on its back doorstep—but had rejected it.

It was no coincidence that the deplorable condition of Union Bay soon inspired new interest in conservation at the university. Under the leadership of Terry Cornelius, the membership of the old Conservation Education and Action Council increased 200 percent and the name of the organization was changed to the Committee for the Environmental Crisis (CEC). The campus, at last, was discovered to be a very real part of the environment, and one which had had its full measure of the crisis.

The climate was right for a confrontation. On campus, construction was being rushed to keep pace with mushrooming enrollment (which hit 33,000 in September 1969). There was immense dissatisfaction with a gargantuan excavation which had destroyed the largest open green area on campus. It came to be nicknamed hatefully "The Pit." In general, people in the university community, and lots of them, were becoming disgusted with the decline of environmental quality and seemed ready to do something personal for their part of nature.

How this latent energy could be harnessed to benefit Union Bay was a question of much concern to us. It answered itself spontaneously one night at a meeting of a new off-campus group called Ecology Action of Puget Sound. We forged a coalition to work together on a common project: an environmental learn-in and fair to be held at the university. While Ecology Action, under the direction of founder David Soucher, was to carry out most of the planning and execution of the event, the CEC was to serve as sponsor and to provide an action event on campus for public participation.

It occurred to me during a campus rap session that a logical and highly demonstrative event might be the establishment of a park on the Union Bay dump. Response to this idea was enthusiastic and heartening. Right then I named it the Union Bay Life-After-Death Resurrection Park, or, for short, the Life Park.

With Jim Lachiotus, details chairman, and several other volunteers, I began working toward the day of the fair and the plant-in. First, we consulted university officials weeks prior to the event to head off the possibility of a student-administration confrontation. We did not, however, construe this consultation as "permission" to carry out the plant-in. I informed the university departments affected that though the plant-in constituted severe public censure of previous management of the land, and though we firmly intended to carry out the plan regardless of university policy, we would nevertheless appreciate their cooperation. Then we circulated a general statement:

> The University failed those of us inside of nature badly when it allowed . . . the ruination of Union Bay Marsh. It has the opportunity now to reclaim some portion . . . of good environmental conscience as well as our respect by supporting and sanctioning the Life Park. If it should be so very insensitive as to resist us in our effort to bring back to the ugly blight of the dump some natural beauty, then . . . the University will be indicted as one of the great, malevolent environmental villains of our time, along with Georgia-Pacific, Kennecott Copper, the pesticide industry, the Vatican and the no-return bottle.

Fortunately, no callousness was encountered. Instead, we were delighted to receive the full cooperation of university officials.

The second matter was to locate a supply of plants. Since it was to be an affair of creation rather than depredation, we could hardly encourage people to dig plants out of their own backyards. Our problem was soon solved by State Lands Commissioner Bert Cole. With Cole's help we were able to purchase conifer seedlings from the State Nursery, which normally sells only to commercial growers.

Dave had color silk-screen posters made to publicize the fair and an additional set especially for the plant-in. Numerous press releases were cranked out and announcements were broadcast by the local radio. By the day of the learn-in plant-in, nearly everyone had been alerted.

The Total Environmental Learn-In Fair (sardonically subtitled "No Deposit-No Return") was a monumental success. It featured a variety of exhibits. A duck decoy bobbed in a tub of crude oil; participants were invited to touch the oil, try to remove it from their hands, then imagine the plight of seabirds with oiled feathers. Displays provided by the Sierra Club, the Audubon Society and other organizations vied for attention with cryptic slide-shows of defoliation in Viet Nam and other environmental crises. The speakers were dynamic and depressingly convincing. They included Brock Evans, Northwest regional Sierra Club representative; Professor Gordan Orians, prominent University of Washington ecologist, and Cliff Humphrey, founder of Ecology Action in Berkeley, among others.

Outside the Student Union building, I mounted the speaker's platform. I did so not without some trepidation, for not once in five years had the subject of a speech from that platform concerned nature's ills. Yet I was buoyed by the fact that the University of Washington *Daily,* which had long shunned conservation as a proper issue for campus concern, had just devoted several columns and an editorial to the fair and the park.

So I rapped about the university environment, and in concluding, I invited the people to march with me to the dump, to help establish our incipient Life Park. Nearly everyone accepted the invitation. The trees, 100 each of Douglas fir, grand fir and ponderosa pine, were handed out. Then we began our half-mile march.

As we crossed intramural playfields, sterile parking lots and the fetid canal that borders the dump, we were met by more marchers. Our ranks included students, faculty, housewives and businessmen, even a high school biology class. Some marchers brought their own plants, including willows, Oregon grape, white pines and one incongruous but welcome bamboo plant. Professor Frank Richardson, resident naturalist, arrived with dozens of shrubs.

We—nearly 400 of us—arrived at the dump at three o'clock in the afternoon. Our negotiations with university personnel had been profitable, for we were greeted with a truckload of topsoil and a couple of dozen shovels. Heads and straights, political activists and ROTC cadets, dug in to plant their own trees, to get their hands in the soil (that topsoil *was* needed, for digging into the cruddy dump dirt a few inches unearthed everything from beer bottles to funny papers). It was heartening to see differences forgotten as one person dug and another lightly tamped fresh soil around fragile roots.

The "resurrection" of Union Bay was over in a couple of hours. Though it seemed to me then that the stench of the dump was less malodorous than before, I realized that our efforts could not end here. Already there were plans for a new university parking lot, an asphalt coffin for a large park-like area next to the ship canal and behind the stadium. We would have to inform the university that the Sequoias and cedars and grass that grace that green expanse could not be sacrificed. And after Life Park, I began to think that the university might listen.

by Brock Evans

Sic 'em, Kids

In the spring of 1969 students and faculty members at Western Washington State College in Bellingham, Washington, faced the kind of problem that conservationists everywhere must face at one time or another: how to compel a congressman to withdraw his support of an environmentally disastrous measure. The measure in this instance was the National Timber Supply Act, which would allow rapid timber-cutting and high-yield techniques in public lands.

The lumber lobby calls the Act a "good conservation bill." Yet it has an altogether different meaning for the Northwest, endowed as it is with more remnants of forested wilderness than remain in any other section of the United States outside of Alaska. Here, tall trees scramble up and down watersheds, circle the bases of high peaks, stand guard along sparkling ice sheets and clear rivers. But the lumber lobby wants to log these forests—here and throughout the national forest system.

One of the original sponsors of the Act was U.S. Representative Lloyd Meeds, a Democrat whose area includes Bellingham. Traditionally, Meeds's environmental voting record had been good. His position supporting the Timber Supply Act therefore came as a surprise to more than a few Washingtonians, including Paul Tholfsen, a young physics instructor at the college,

---

Brock Evans is the Sierra Club's staff representative in the Northwest.

and Al Doan, student body president. Tholfsen and
Doan sat right down and wrote themselves a fact sheet.
Then Tholfsen bought 100 five-cent postcards and,
armed with mimeographed copies of the fact sheet, the
two set up a card table outside the Student Union.
"Invest 5¢ in Wilderness," their placard urged.

"We just sat back," recalls Tholfsen. "Pretty soon
students and professors began crowding around to see
what it was all about. The first response after reading
our fact sheet was disbelief and anger. Their second
reaction was to buy a postcard." Within three days,
nearly 400 cards had been sold, annotated with comments of outrage, and posted to Congressman Meeds's
office. Four hundred postcards on a single issue is a
lot of mail to cross any congressman's desk. Mr. Meeds
soon withdrew his name from the list of the Timber
Supply Act's sponsors.

Some months later, in Oregon, students mobilized
again in defense of trees.

Eugene, it should be noted, is "the lumber capital of
the world," or at least that's what the local chamber of
commerce claims. And the U.S. Department of Agriculture has a Forest Service unit based in Eugene that
is eager to encourage that claim. Over the years, it has
sanctioned widespread cutting of virgin timber: of some
70 major valleys in the Oregon Cascades, only three
remain untouched by the saw. One of these rare and
special places is the valley of French Pete Creek.

Several years ago, the Forest Service decided French
Pete should be logged, too. But opposition from con-
servation groups bought the big trees some time. The
Forest Service backed off. The loggers lobbied. Seesaw.
Before long, French Pete was up for logging again.

Then came Nature's Conspiracy, a new student organization at the University of Oregon in Eugene. One
of the Conspiracy's first moves was to pull together
some 1,500 students and community residents for a
march on the Forest Service's headquarters. When the
marchers arrived there, the forest supervisor refused
to meet with them. So they deposited seedlings at his

front door as a symbol of what would be needed at
French Pete Creek if the loggers were allowed to cut
in the valley.

"Sic 'em, Kids," the local press said approvingly.
And before long the Forest Service announced another
"delay" in its French Pete plan. This gave conservationists time to file legal appeals. The valley may yet be
saved.

And so may the other wildlands of the Northwest be
saved—as long as the young activists of Bellingham and
Eugene hang in there. And sic 'em.

by Allan Planz

The Pool

On the west bank of brown river there is a place where
the wildness of nature mingles savagely with the wildness of civilization. Bare rocks have shouldered the rain
into a sunken meadow, and more than a dozen auto-
bodies create a ring of metallic resonance around the
small pond, from which all life, even the mosquito
wriggler, has been choked by chemical stasis. Sunlight
sickens on rust and purpled alloys, glints on the black
water and shimmers on oilstained sand. This was a
watering place once, a ford, a concourse, and one of
many thousands of departure points. Buffalo rested by
the rocks, heads to the wind, and geese held back the
encroaching swamp for centuries, until guns killed off
the geese and later gasoline killed the weeds. The
erosion gulley was a stream when lush grasses upcoun-
try sifted the rain through their roots. Now every drizzle
means sudden flood. Here Indians made camp near the
bank, and watched the fire shape and shadow the
waters. The pioneer paused to collect his forces for the
plunge farther into the west on the trail which, under
moonlight, stirred faintly above the dark. A family
settled here, and built a homestead, of which only a few
rectangular depressions remain. This land was over-
grazed, overfarmed, and abandoned, then assumed a
civilized function as a dumping-ground for vandalized
carwrecks from the highway a mile off. Though doubt-

Allan Planz is poetry editor of *The Nation*.

less title to it is jealously guarded, nobody possesses it now, nobody watches over it, and it is nameless. One can come across it hiking and descend the rocks to the black pond and rest among the junked cars and among slaughtered beasts. Locusts skid in the sand or sing, entombed, in the sticky sludge spilled from crankcases. The river with its machined flow scours the pocked bank. The shadows inside and under the cars are bruises of blue air. Dustdevils snake in the fine grit, and whirl flakes of rusted metal. One may calculate and possess again all the miles he has traveled, all the cities and towns that he called home and that irresistibly erupted him back on the road. One may calculate all those whom money had bought, or killed. One may do nothing, wish nothing. If the hot breeze stirs, it brings only the hands of buried men, and bears no witness to the riposte of osprey and eagle above terraces of clear water. And the night comes on, upside down, gaining on the earth a darkness it never has in the sky. The air smells of heated iron, rancid oils, and of water thickened with sewage. Voices in the blood begin talking of the blood's cessation. One picks up a theme, then, of the splendor of empire weighted against the dust of the people who built it.

And gives it to the heaviness of the night through which one has lived each night, getting drunk under stars arranged in patterns long since prefigured in the fears of men. And with the geophysics of the night in one hand, a bottle in the other, invokes that theme, so that, when the dawn splays the broken figure of man or beast on a hilltop, the wind may come again, if ever it comes again, singing not requiem but revolution.

PART V

the law

"Human society must exist within a framework of law, or exist not at all."

by James S. Rummonds

A Challenge to the Law

Until recently, the legal community, like so many other segments of U.S. society, failed to recognize the critical condition of our environment. It had traditionally followed concepts germinated during the Industrial Revolution and nurtured in the fertile soil of American technology. Experts abound in the fields of tax dodge, corporate merger, and labor law. Everyone has heard of oil and gas law, tort law and criminal law. But whoever heard of environmental law? How many students have been supplied the tools with which to win court battles over environmental polluters? Giving little or no thought to whose interests they best represented, or the consequences of that representation, law school graduates happily dove into the pot of gold at the end of the rainbow. Such was the lawyer's American dream.

Now, everywhere, the cry "save our ship" can be heard. Our ship, of course, is the spaceship earth upon which we all must travel. Politicians now realize that elections may be decided by the extent of their environmental concern, and are, therefore, expressing a good deal of it. In the congressional elections of 1970, "we the people" will have been the first to make a national, political issue of disgraceful environmental damage.

Not only the legal profession has failed to recognize our environmental problems, and not only the military-industrial complex has created them. We all are guilty

---

James S. Rummonds is a law student at Stanford University.

of complicity in bringing about the present level of environmental destruction. Yet, we must ask ourselves: What can we do to ward off that destruction? What role can the law play? For human society must exist within a framework of law, or exist not at all. Once, man's refusal to deal with the public's best interests resulted only in isolated repercussions; today such refusal cannot be condoned. Our survival depends on which interests we choose to serve—on recognizing mankind's long-range interests as the paramount ones, and acting accordingly.

In the past, we demanded goods, and got them. The law and economics shaped a process which both satisfied consumer demand and made profits for the manufacturer. Now, there are encouraging signs that consumers are demanding different products: clean air, pure water and a quality environment. If democracy actually works, it should be easy to transfer these consumer demands into the political arena.

The legal profession not only represents the people before the law, but to a large extent creates the rules by which we live. Therefore, it is critical that the legal community recognize the public interest, promote that recognition and work toward a program that reflects it.

One major default of the law has been its general ignorance of environmental regulations. There is little real expertise in environmental litigation. Within American law schools few courses have been offered to fill this void. In short, the challenge to the legal community is a great one.

Citizens' ignorance of legal rights and recourses is a pervasive problem. Additionally, the people who most need legal assistance usually don't have the funds to hire attorneys. Those attorneys who contribute their time are limited by their professional duties.

Last year several law students at Stanford organized the Environmental Law Society (ELS) to bring the research skills and creative energy of law students to bear, in the manner of legal aid societies, on environmental issues. We immediately discovered tremendous enthusiasm for the program among students, the law school faculty, and the administration as well. Some sixty students joined the ELS. The Legal Aid Society, several faculty members, and the dean's office helped give us an initial push.

What can an environmental law society do to solve environmental problems?

First, it can contribute factual research. Solutions often depend on the quality and quantity of factual evidence that can be marshaled, especially in legislative, administrative and regulatory efforts to determine policies and standards. State legislatures, for example, which are generally overworked, understaffed, and inadequately financed, heavily depend on factual information. Often that information is readily available to law students. Recently a California legislative committee needed information on the composition and representation of local planning agencies to draw up an open space preservation plan for metropolitan areas. Lacking the necessary resources, the committee requested assistance from the Stanford ELS, whose members conducted field research and put together a report that will be used by the committee in formulating a state-wide open space policy.

Institutional research is another area where contributions can be made. Certain questions need answering: What are the powers and authorities of local planning bodies vis-a-vis the state, the county, and regional bodies? How are these powers limited, and how best utilized? What sanctions are available to them? Whose interests are being represented and protected? Many of the answers can be found by law students. Such efforts can be undertaken on a broad scale.

Even after institutional and factual research has been completed, much is left for the ELS to do. There is the job of persuading a decision-making agency to adopt solutions. That effort can involve aiding attorneys, testifying before regulatory agencies and government bodies, lobbying, and publicizing problems and solutions. In addition to state legislatures, local agencies, municipal corporations, citizens' groups, and private individuals all encounter similar problems and require similar assistance.

The overwhelming need for legal contributions warrants a major national effort on the part of law students. Toward this end in the fall of 1969, the National Environmental Law Society was organized at Stanford to coordinate efforts of various local societies and agitate for organization at schools not yet involved. Within a few quick months, contact was made with many law schools throughout the country. Participating schools now include Harvard, Yale, Columbia, and George Washington universities; the universities of Pennsylvania, Virginia, Michigan, Chicago, Texas, Denver, Utah, Washington, and Oregon; Willamette University; Hastings; the University of California at Davis, Berkeley, and Los Angeles, and the University of Southern California.

In addition to coordinating local efforts, the national ELS will publish a newsletter (to keep each group informed about the others' activity) and an Environmental Law Review. It will sponsor environmental law conferences, and establish a reporting system and case file available to all. The ultimate goal of the national organization is the establishment of a nationwide network for volunteer legal research assistance available to everyone, from United States congressmen to private citizens.

Law students cannot achieve these goals alone. They will need the assistance of the law schools where they can be sensitized to environmental issues, given the tools to deal with them, and allowed to test their legal education by confronting real problems on a working level. Law schools can offer courses dealing with relevant environmental issues (as Stanford has done for the past year), encourage the development of student organizations like the ELS, make available faculty expertise, assist in publishing relevant material, offer credit for significant work projects in heretofore extra-curricular areas, institute interdisciplinary studies, and make arrangements to hold Continuing Education of the Bar courses for the benefit of practicing, interested, attorneys. The value of these programs could hardly be challenged.

Beyond the campus, a sort of community environmental A.C.L.U. should be established to complement each ELS chapter. The lawyers could call on the students for research assistance, donate a certain amount of their time toward directing student efforts, supply practical information on how to organize community support and promote political action. Many such groups are already forming around the country.

These legal innovations would seem to constitute a new, powerful weapon in the fight for a better environment. At Stanford, the weapon was soon put to the test.

Shortly after its debut, the ELS began receiving requests for assistance from all over the country. One request came from a gentleman who claimed that Stanford University itself was playing a major part in the desecration of the foothills on the San Francisco peninsula by expanding its 550-acre industrial park into undeveloped Coyote Hill. We responded by calling a meeting of interested parties. Students, lawyers, representatives from the Sierra Club, the Palo Alto Civic League, the Los Altos Hills Association, Committee for Green Foothills, United Stanford Employees Housing Committee, and the Stanford Conservation Group attended. Our first order of business was to examine background events leading up to the university's expansion into Coyote Hill.

Civic and conservation groups have been concerned for years about the disposition of 9,400 acres of Stanford's open space land in the foothills behind Palo Alto: the university had annexed a considerable acreage from adjacent municipalities for such non-academic purposes as industrial, commercial, and residential use. Conservation-minded people maintained that Stanford evaded its responsibility to the public by ignoring the overall effects of its industrial development, and by setting a poor example for the rest of the community. Earlier university development had created traffic problems, caused new roads to be built through residential areas (adding to a critical shortage of low-income housing), and condemned other open space land to asphalt and concrete.

Of course, it is hardly fair to condemn Stanford University alone for wanting to increase its revenues to educate more students, better. The university's actions in this case simply reflected a pervasive illness of our society. Underlying the Coyote Hill dispute was a long-standing, intense dedication to the development ethic. Development for its own sake has always been considered a good thing. Although we could hold Stanford to a higher standard, it should be emphasized that the university is no worse than some and considerably better than many similarly situated American power structures, especially in view of the corporate representation of its Board of Trustees, which reads like a *Who's Who* of the American Industrial State: Hewlett-Packard, Lockheed, Bank of America, General Dynamics, Utah Construction Company, Arcata National Corporation, and Ducommon Corporation.

Palo Alto has for years seemed to view its welfare as consistent with that of Stanford University. To promote the smooth functioning of such a mutually profitable partnership, there are generally a few strategically placed persons who appear to owe allegiance to two masters. A member of the university business office sits on the board of directors of an important construction company which has done considerable work in the Stanford Industrial Park. Another member of the same office sits on the Palo Alto City Council and votes on matters of deep concern to his employer. However, such relationships are not unusual; they probably exist in city councils, planning commissions, and regulatory agencies in every city and town in the country.

In examining the events behind the decision to

develop Coyote Hill, the ELS was able to focus on several promising-looking legal issues.

One issue concerned the way in which the area had been subdivided. Stanford originally had submitted a Tentative Map of Lot Division Under Five Lots (actually four lots) of the area. This procedure did not require Planning Commission approval or City Council hearings open to the public. After the Tentative Map had been approved by the city (without prior notice to the Commission), Stanford commenced road construction. Later, the university further subdivided these lots into more easily leasable parcels. The second subdivision had the benefit of full hearings and was approved by a split 5 to 4 vote.

These events raised a number of questions:

Did Stanford circumvent the city's Subdivision Ordinance by undertaking the first subdivision without seeking regular City Council approval, while fully intending to subdivide the same area further?

Did two Palo Alto City councilmen engage in a conflict of interest by voting for the second Coyote Hill subdivision? At issue is whether or not the councilman from the Stanford business office could vote for or against his employer's interest with objectivity. The second councilman is a partner in a construction company which, at the time of the vote, intended to submit bids on Coyote Hill contracts. This issue will soon be decided by the California Conflict of Interest Statute, which some authorities think is unfortunately more form than substance.

Did the Planning Director of the City of Palo Alto violate a city ordinance by failing to notify the City Council of the first Coyote Hill subdivision during the nine months after it was submitted to him? At issue is whether or not the official was required to report *all* subdivision decisions or simply the final one.

Each of the above questions was thoroughly researched by members of the Stanford ELS. At the next meeting of the "Friends of Coyote Hill," the decision was made to bring suit against the university. The complaint was accordingly filed in the Palo Alto Branch of the Superior Court of the State of California a few short hours before the running out of the statute of limitations. It asks, as a remedy, for a declaratory judgment that all city proceedings were invalid and void, and for a permanent injunction to prevent Stanford from developing any of the Coyote Hill property.

The defendants have filed a "demurrer" which alleges that the plaintiff's causes of action do not state facts sufficient to constitute a cause of action. The demurrer alleges that the applicable subdivision act and ordinances say nothing about "intent." It further alleges that City Council approval of the subsequent subdivision was valid because neither of the two Councilmen had a "disabling" conflict of interest.

The Coyote Hill case is now before the court; at this writing, we can only await its judgment.

Whatever the outcome of this case, it may be of secondary importance only. More important is the attention newly focused on "whose interest is served," and on where and how the public's interest fits into the total picture, and on the formation of a positive working relationship between members of the legal community.

Thus have law students initiated efforts to bring their special skills to focus on the problem of inadequately regulated industrial expansion. At Stanford, and other law schools around the country, faculty and administration have given their enthusiastic cooperation.

Law students everywhere are showing concern in many areas not traditionally dealt with by the law. Many law schools are already adapting to these changing attitudes by integrating formulas for social change into the legal curriculum. The area of environmental law is only one such area, but a critical one. The plan I have outlined (while incomplete and needing revision) affords the law the opportunity to play a significant role in one of the greatest challenges confronting mankind. The plan is no panacea but it is a decent beginning. It is also a positive indication that the law has risen to the environmental challenge.

by Chet Atkins and Wendy Kimball

State Legislatures: The Next Target

The focus for environmental reform is on Washington, D.C. The pressure is on Congress. But who is pressing the fight in the 50 other legislatures? Who speaks for a quality environment on the state level? Too often, unhappily, the answer is—no one.

Environmental upkeep has been, by default, a traditionally federal enterprise. With each new Congress, conservation groups have begun anew the search for sympathetic federal legislators. Reform measures are launched on slow, circuitous, and often unsuccessful journeys through Capitol Hill, while petitions to Executive departments seldom receive substantial attention.

Where can an environmental reform movement with limited funds make its greatest legislative impact? Certain environmental problems, such as toxic emissions from automobiles, can of course be controlled most effectively by the federal government. But often other problems—industrial waste disposal or the depletion of open spaces—demand solution at the level of the state. State government officials, furthermore, are generally more accessible than their federal counterparts. In some cases, they may be easier to reach than the boys down at City Hall.

In a Congressional district of, say, 400,000 people,

Chet Atkins and Wendy Kimball are majoring in political science at Antioch College.

the average citizen is usually not equipped to attract
his Congressman's attention, much less persuade the
Representative to take a strong position on a controver-
sial issue. At the other extreme, local government
offices, paradoxically, can be difficult to penetrate. It is
not uncommon for local officials to be closely allied
with the very industries blocking environmental reform.

Though the state legislator may have similar allies,
at least he has fewer constituents than the Congressman.
Thus, a letter addressed to him is more likely to receive
his personal attention. And it needn't end with a letter.
There are many ways by which a citizen can ensure that
his suggestion receives serious legislative consideration.

One of the avenues open to residents of some states
is the citizen's petition to the legislature. A citizen's
petition, for example, can require a state representative
or senator to submit to the legislature any measure requested by an adult resident of his state. The initial
tactic is to ask a sympathetic legislator to sponsor and
file your proposed measure before the deadline of the
upcoming legislative session. As its sponsor, the representative or senator will have your petition redrafted
as a bill. Then it will travel the route of all bills, through
committee hearings to floor debate and final action.
Many states permit public hearings on each bill in committee, during which any individual may present testimony. By organizing groups of citizens to present convincing testimony before a committee, supporters of a
bill can further the public interest in it and build legislative support. Professional experts in such fields as
ecology or medicine can be particularly convincing before statehouse committees. A favorable committee
report, needless to say, will enhance the bill's position
when it reaches the floor of the legislature.

Bringing an issue to the statehouse can have beneficial effects even if the measure inspired by it does not
actually pass. For example, a pending bill can become a
rallying point for other reformers throughout the state.
Even the short life of an innovative but unsuccessful

bill can, at the very least, be used to arouse interest in neglected issues. Such exposure forces otherwise disinterested legislators to inform themselves, and press coverage passes much of this information on to the public. If the bill is rejected after heated legislative battles and wide public exposure, reforms may still be forthcoming, even as certain defeated antipollution measures have stimulated industries to begin long-overdue research on more efficient engines, cleaner fuels and biodegradable detergents.

The potential impact of any piece of reform legislation, however, depends on the energy and expertise of its supporters. Thorough press coverage is essential, since most state legislators are prone to associate themselves favorably with widely publicized popular issues. Freshman legislators, eager to establish reputations, often respond to groups that can demonstrate skillful and effective handling of innovative legislation. Other legislators may be pressured into supporting environmental reform if it becomes known that their seats may otherwise be challenged by popular supporters of conservation.

Of course, the bill itself must first be carefully prepared. Adaptable laws or bills from other states, and actual or pending federal legislation accompanied by committee reports can provide helpful guidelines.

In December, 1969, we filed a citizen's petition in Massachusetts to restrict the sale of non-biodegradable detergents, which are common sources of pollution in freshwater areas. On the federal level, a similar bill has been introduced by Senator Gaylord Nelson of Wisconson. Our petition is pending.

A dispute between local residents concerned with the preservation of wetlands in one author's home town (Concord, Massachusetts) led last year to another petition. We asked the state legislature to establish an environmental control board to report on the ecological effects of all planned projects costing over $500,000. Although this proposed board would not have the power to veto a project, its reports would alert private action groups to any projects that might threaten environmental quality. This, too, is pending.

A third petition was inspired recently by a radio broadcast about illnesses suffered by bridge and tunnel toll collectors in New York City. Our petition would require installation of carbon monoxide meters in toll booths along the Massachusetts Turnpike, and evacuation of the toll collectors when the emissions reached a near-toxic level. Like the other measures, however, this petition has not yet reached the floor of the legislature.

Even a bill with broad public support can be rejected or neutralized when certain procedural considerations are neglected. The following questions should always be kept in mind:

- Is the measure legal under the state and federal constitutions?
- Does it conflict with existing legislation?
- Can its provisions be twisted in any way to weaken the interest of environmental control?
- Does the agency designated to execute the bill as law have the power to enforce it?
- Are adequate funds available to administer the measure? (Nullification of a law through inadequate appropriations is common on the federal level. The unanimously-passed Clean Water Restoration Act of 1966 authorized $1 billion for sewage treatment in 1970, but the Administration budgeted only $214 million. Only after a fight by a handful of Congressmen was the full $1 billion item restored.)

While the guidelines offered here have dealt with action at the state level, it must be understood that the opportunity for citizen participation in legislative processes at *all* levels of government is unlimited and must be exploited. Rather than be disheartened by the traditional indifference of legislators, environmentalists should be encouraged by the increasing public support for their efforts. The way it's shaping up, environmental indifference will soon be a luxury legislators can ill afford.

by David Peter Sachs

Saving San Francisco Bay— in Sacramento

Nobody saved San Francisco Bay. Everybody did. Its rescue from commercial filling and exploitation was accomplished by a combination of student and public pressure groups working with a legal, legislative policy team. The events of January-July, 1969, dramatized a most precedent-setting battle in public affairs policy-making, and, hopefully, ushered in an Environmental Era in California.

From 1851, when the State of California first sold beach property along San Francisco Bay to the City of San Francisco, much of the Bay has been touched by the filler's shovel. As the city grew and needed port facilities closer to the deeper channel water, what could be simpler than filling in more mud flats to get there? Because it was much more economical to build on flat land than on hilly terrain, what could make better sense than knocking a few hills into the tidelands? The reclaimed Bay area would make good flat building land, too. And since salt marshes are a waste of space, why not dike them off to turn them into salt evaporators, and when that is no longer economical, just add some more fill and build houses on it?

David Peter Sachs is a medical student at Stanford University and president of the Stanford chapter of the Student American Medical Association.

In little more than one hundred years, the shape of the Bay has changed drastically. A multitude of fill projects, initiated by cities, corporations, land speculators, county, state and Federal governments, nibbled away at the Bay shoreline. By 1958, the water-to-land conversion had reduced the area of the Bay from 680 to 437 square miles. At this rate, by 2020 only 120 square miles would remain, and the Bay would have to be renamed the San Francisco River.

Intelligent observers began to speculate that without the expanse of Bay, San Francisco's pleasant year-round climate eventually would change to one of torrid heat, much like that of the Central California Valley. And the loss of smog-controlling water plants, and Bay water itself, might bring the area under continual gas-mask alert.

Consequently in the late Fifties and early Sixties, pressure mounted for a comprehensive plan to govern use and development of the Bay. In those days, "three dowagers and a disc jockey," as one insider phrased it, instigated public concern. As a result of the efforts of the Save San Francisco Bay Association (headed by Mrs. Clark Kerr, Sylvia McLaughlin and Esther Gulick), disc jockey Don Sherwood, Assemblyman Nicholas Petris, and others, the San Francisco Bay Conservation Study Commission came into being in 1964. It received three assignments: to undertake a study to ascertain the public interest in San Francisco Bay, to determine the effects of further filling "upon navigation, fish, and wildlife, air and water pollution, and all of the regional needs of the future population," and to report to the 1965 Legislature with recommended legislation.

The report which the Study Commission released in January, 1965, recognized that the Bay must be treated as a total regional entity free from piecemeal control (nine counties and more than 77 municipalities border the Bay). It recommended that a 29-member Bay Conservation and Development Commission (BCDC) be established, composed of representatives from Federal, state, city and county governments and the general public, to present to the State Legislature by January 1969 a "comprehensive plan for conservation and use of the Bay and development of its shoreline." Most importantly, the report recommended the BCDC have *complete* control over all fill projects in San Francisco Bay. The BCDC was established, and went to work.

After four years of public hearings, scientific studies, and legislative preparation, the BCDC released its 134-page *San Francisco Bay Plan* along with a 572-page supplement of supporting technical data. The BCDC Bay Plan recommended establishment of a permanent Bay Conservation and Development Commission which would halt speculative fill and real estate development projects totaling millions of dollars. Unless the State Legislature put it on a permanent basis, the Commission and its regulatory authority were to disappear 90 days after the close of the 1969 legislative session. Fill projects could then proceed with impunity.

The developers, primarily the Leslie Salt Company, Santa Fe Railroad, and Westbay Associates (a combine composed of the Chase Manhattan Bank and David Rockefeller in New York, along with the Crocker Citizens Bank and Ideal Cement Company of California) had millions to lose and millions to back their fight. They were counting on many old friends in the Senate, in particular those on the Senate's Governmental Efficiency Committee, to kill all Bay-saving legislation. In January, 1969, the prognosis for San Francisco Bay was not good.

But developers did not know then that a revolution was fermenting on the Senate floor and that many allegiances were soon to change. Key senators would be confronted by an angry, insistent constituency. Younger senators would become increasingly disturbed by the "old guard." Conservationists would draw upon unusual legal and lobbying expertise.

A group of five people from the Sierra Club, the San Francisco Planning and Conservation League, and the Save the Bay Association joined to form a conservationists' legislative policy team. With the exception of John Zierold (an experienced, full-time lobbyist for the Planning and Conservation League), the team virtually left their professional work in the Bay area to establish a lobbying base in Sacramento. Practicing attorneys Dwight Steele, Peter Behr, and Herbert Rubin, and Will Siri (Sierra Club past president) were old hands at state politics and knew enough to expect trouble from the Senate old guard. Specifically, for years environmentalists had watched Senate President Pro-Tem Hugh Burns funnel good legislation that would logically be dealt with by the Natural Resources Committee into Senator Richard Dolwig's Governmental Efficiency Committee, where it disappeared, never to be seen again. Fortunately, many of the younger senators, who had watched bills meet this Venus's-flytrap doom in the Dolwig Committee, were determined to break that chain.

Zierold and the legislative policy team were sure of enough support to put a "skeleton bill" into the Natural Resources Committee which they would then use as an ace in the hole if strong Bay control bills by Assemblyman John Knox and Senator Nicholas Petris got stuck in Governmental Efficiency. The team knew that if a strong bill ever reached the Senate floor, sufficient support existed there to pass it.

Basically, the Knox Bill transferred the entire BCDC *San Francisco Bay Plan* into law. But the old guard in the Senate, and the developers, desired either complete dissolution of the Bay Conservation and Development Commission or an emasculated *Bay Plan* which would allow unrestricted filling once again.

Throughout most of the winter and spring, it appeared that once the Knox Bill left the Assembly it would never leave the Governmental Efficiency Committee. So Senator George Moscone introduced a skeleton bill to restore a provision in the State Natural Resource Code that a county must have a land-use master plan before it could acquire beach property. Although seemingly of little relevance in saving the Bay, it was highly germane, for beach and shoreline controls

were central issues in the *Bay Plan*. The skeleton bill
provided an ideal framework on which to hang relevant
legislation. The master plan issue served as an ideal
cover for a strong BCDC bill.

Although Senator Dolwig's opposition to the Knox
and Petris Bills (embodying the *Bay Plan*) was voci-
ferous, citizen pressure in his home district of San Mateo
County began to mount. Mrs. Claire Dedrick and Janet
Adams, Rodney Minot and Mrs. Eleanor Boushey
formed the Save Our Bay Action Committee which
proceeded to stir up one of the most impressive public
showings of support for any bill. Working with some 50
other Bay area organizations and student groups like
ours at Stanford, they showered shopping centers and
train stations with leaflets explaining the Knox and
Petris Bills and urging citizens to write or cable Senator
Dolwig's office. Some 37,000 brilliant blue "Save Our
Bay" bumper stickers were distributed by groups of
students, and Sierra Club chapters.

Even to the most dull-witted observer, it was obvious
that the Bay was fast becoming as sacred as apple pie.
Citizen pressure began to change Senator Dolwig's approach to Bay legislation. He introduced his own bill to
"save" the Bay, one which would actually have the
opposite effect. He proposed a new commission (to go
into operation as if the BCDC had never existed)
charged with developing over a five-year period pre-
cisely the same guidelines as those in the Knox Bill.
This ploy may have been intended to confuse the public
into thinking that the light had been seen and the Bay
was safe.

Press releases and public information bulletins from
the Save Our Bay Action Committee, the Save the Bay
Association, and the Sierra Club kept emphasizing that
the Knox and Petris Bills presented the only viable plan.
On April 19, 1969, the Save Our Bay Action Committee placed a full-page, two-color advertisement in
several Bay area newspapers: "There is no time for
tomorrow! Today, demand of Senator Richard J.
Dolwig (R-San Mateo County), Chairman, Govern-

mental Efficiency Committee, the removal of his own bill, S.B. 893—and any other bill designed to exploit San Francisco Bay and its shorelines—from consideration by his Governmental Efficiency Committee of the Legislature of the State of California . . ."

Then, the various conservation groups, including the Stanford Conservation Group, which had mobilized a coterie of active high school students, developed a double-pronged petition expressing support of the Knox-Petris Bill and demanding withdrawal of all others from the Senate. One petition was addressed to Governor Ronald Reagan and the other to Senator Dolwig. This tactic reaped fantastic publicity.

Throughout early spring, the petition campaign grew and public sentiment for the BCDC increased. Simultaneously, some incredibly outlandish plans were proposed for Bay development. Westbay Associates suggested a massive conveyor system to transport thousands of cubic yards of the San Bruno Mountains (located two miles south of San Francisco) over the Bayshore Freeway and to dump the earth into the Bay and waiting barges. (The barges would facilitate land fill at other Bay locations.)

By the end of April, public opinion was beginning to stack up against Senator Dolwig. Prominent Republican fund raisers from his district stated openly that if a strong Bay bill did not pass, they would seek out another Republican candidate to support in the 1970 election. Dolwig's Sacramento office had been deluged with thousands of telephone calls, telegrams, and letters demanding his support for the Knox bill. Full-page ads continued in Bay area newspapers. News releases poured out of conservation offices. For 20 days in May delegations from cities in the senator's district personally delivered thousands of petitions containing more than 280,000 signatures to his Sacramento office. Late in the spring, the matching petition to Governor Reagan was dramatically deposited on the Capitol steps. Reportedly, telephone calls from California's Republican Congressmen in Washington to Reagan's office made it clear that if California did not permanently protect San Francisco Bay, they were prepared to introduce Federal legislation to do the job. Consequently, the Governor warned, "We cannot permit a lapse, no matter how short, in the protection of this priceless natural resource."

Senator Dolwig then changed his own bill to parallel the Knox-Petris legislation, but insisted he had not done so "because of 60,000 clamoring women." The campaign also had a crucial effect on other senators who could easily imagine their constituencies mounting a similar effort against them. Many borderline legislators became favorably inclined toward strong Bay legislation.

Meanwhile, the conservationists' legislative policy team in Sacramento continued to work overtime. Public support had strengthened their bargaining position but victory was not in sight. President Pro-Tem Burns would unquestionably send the Knox Bill to the Governmental Efficiency Committee where old guard senators could make certain it moved no further.

In May, Senator Moscone's skeleton bill quietly moved out of the Senate into Assemblyman George Milias's Natural Resources Committee, where Milias had agreed to sit on it until the fate of the Knox Bill was certain. That is, if the Knox Bill were squelched by the Governmental Efficiency Committee, Milias's committee would amend the skeleton bill to incorporate the entire *San Francisco Bay Plan*.

As it happened, this wasn't necessary because late spring events on the Senate floor suddenly changed the entire picture for Bay legislation. A revolt of young senators, which developed faster than anyone had thought possible, led to the ouster of Burns and the election of ecologically-oriented Howard Way as President Pro-Tem of the Senate. After Way's installation and the entry of the Knox Bill into the Senate, Way sent it to the Local Government Committee, from which it eventually emerged with additions that made it even stronger than when it had passed from the Assembly to the Senate.

At the time of Way's election, the Governmental Efficiency Committee was sitting on five Bay control bills of varying strength, sponsored by Senators John McCarthy, Milton Marks, Nicholas Petris (essentially identical to the Knox Bill), John Nejedly, and Richard Dolwig (the much-revised S.B. 839). Without debate, Governmental Efficiency passed these out into the Finance Committee whose membership was similar to Governmental Efficiency's. So when the Knox Bill arrived at the Finance Committee, it was one of *six* Bay control bills under consideration.

Meanwhile, throughout July, caravans of buses carried thousands of people to the Sacramento hearings to support a strong Bay bill. And the earlier effect of public concern on Senator Dolwig (who was now working for a strong bill) had not been lost on other senators. The result was that the Finance Committee created its own new bill, a coalition Knox-Marks-Petris-Dolwig Bill, which was basically the same as the original, strong, Knox Bill.

Many of the conservative members of the Finance Committee did their best to weaken it: two cities were granted exemptions for current fill projects, and a key provision giving BCDC control over shoreline development was removed. But public pressure and pressure from President Pro-Tem Way saved the bill from being pigeonholed, and it was moved out to the Senate floor.

On the floor, environmental lobbyists used all their diplomatic skills to reinstate the shoreline control provision. After several days, and a flurry of quorum calls, they succeeded. Further amendments to weaken the bill were defeated. One example was Senator John McCarthy's floor amendment to reduce the number of commission votes required to alter the BCDC Plan from a two-thirds vote to a simple majority. As this change could have laid the BCDC wide open for developers, it was vitally important to defeat the amendment.

Senator McCarthy introduced his amendment late one day, when there were only a few senators on the floor. The amendment was defeated. But then, he made a crucial mistake: he did not move for reconsideration. According to Senate rules, an amendment may not be introduced twice without a motion for reconsideration at the time of defeat. Conservation lobbyist Zierold noticed McCarthy's error.

The following day McCarthy tried to reintroduce the amendment. The conservation lobbyists' legislative counsel cited the Senate reconsideration rules. Taken by surprise, the McCarthy forces moved to suspend the rules. But the conservationists working with Senator Petris had seen to it that all of their supporters were in the Senate, and requested a quorum call. The move to suspend the rules, which would have allowed reconsideration of the McCarthy amendment, was defeated because the opposition could not get enough votes to the floor in time. It was a sweet victory for the conservationists.

On August 1, 1969, the Knox-Marks-Petris-Dolwig coalition bill (A.B. 2057) passed the Senate with a vote of 22 to 9. Governor Reagan signed it into law on August 7.

What makes a successful campaign?

Pressure brought to bear by citizen's groups was crucial in securing passage of the comprehensive BCDC bill. The Save Our Bay Action Committee achieved amazing results with expenditures totaling $53,000. That sum included $26,000 for one statewide advertisement, $5,000 for other newspaper ads, $2,500 for bumper stickers, $3,000 for postage and the balance for secretarial services, duplicating expenses, telephone, etc. More than 300,000 pages of mimeographed and printed material were distributed, some handed out by high school and college students, others mailed to membership lists generously furnished by such organizations as Rotary, Kiwanis, and Sierra groups. Workers canvassed the Bay area for endorsements from groups such as the Bay Area Central Labor Council. But probably the single most effective technique was the constant stream of press releases which meant instant exposure several times a day to thousands of people.

Important as public pressure is, it is not sufficient to secure a bill's passage. A piece of legislation must be constantly watchdogged. Therefore it is vital to have as many full-time lobbyists as possible. The more skillful, knowledgeable, and articulate they are, the more effective they will be in securing passage of environmental measures. But without strong and well-publicized support from the public, lobbyists cannot accomplish much.

Certain crucial events cannot be planned in advance. Perhaps the most important single factor in the entire save-the-Bay battle was the replacement of conservative President Pro-Tem Burns by liberal Howard Way. Without this replacement, it is possible that the only result of months of citizen effort and lobbying would have been an alienation and disillusionment with the democratic process.

Creating and passing a bill is a very human, interpersonal phenomenon. Assemblyman Knox's bill and the man himself were tremendously influential. The bill has been described as one of the most solid and leakproof ever to sail the twisted channels of the legislature. Assemblyman Knox, a lawyer, was a strong advocate; he presented highly articulate arguments before committees and the public. One of his key staffers, Tom Willoughby, continually worked with the conservationists' legislative policy team.

In any active, eco-political campaign, many people must make considerable personal sacrifices and alter their own priorities. The passage of the Knox Bill required an intricate combination of events which, through planning and luck, all occurred in the right place, at the right time.

Those 20 days in May have generated on-going political repercussions. Burns's ouster acted as a catalyst for the formation of a Democratic-Republican coalition. Several conservative senators are now finding, for the first time in decades, stiff district opposition in the forthcoming election, resulting from *their* original opposition to a strong Bay bill.

A most significant piece of environmental legislation has become a reality. Only time will tell if the citizens of the region will allow this law to save the great Bay of San Francisco, for all time.

PART VI

the media

"Hard sell Mad-Ave overkill is not necessary. The problem is not so much *getting* publicity but *coping* with it."

by John Zeh

Getting into Print

Having a journalist on the program of the UNESCO environment conference last fall was not so unusual, because this particular journalist—Wolf Von Eckhardt —specializes in architecture and all of its ecological interrelations. But Von Eckhardt did not limit his remarks to building design and new-city concepts. Instead, he took on the nation's newspapers, criticizing them for mishandling one of their biggest stories: the environmental crisis. Newspapers treat the environment in a fragmented fashion, he charged. They report a housing project here and a transportation crisis there, rarely pointing out that misplaced housing will only worsen the transportation situation. "Today's newspapers are just as complacent about the environment as they were about the ghetto, and for similar reasons," Von Eckhardt noted. "And we as a result are half ignorant and half indifferent."

What Von Eckhardt had to say about the commercial media applies also to campus newspapers, and to their college readers. Until the current ecology movement gained strength, most campus editors knew little about destruction of the environment, or didn't care. The environment was handled like the war in its early years. "What's going on over there doesn't directly concern this campus or its students, so it's not news," isolationist

John Zeh is editor of *Moderator* Magazine, a national campus bimonthly.

editors would proclaim. "Women's hours and cafeteria food are more 'relevant' to our readers. We only have so much space." Student editors soon woke up to the "relevance" of the war and other "off-campus" issues and began offering news coverage and editorial comment. Now, the environment is getting play in the campus press, too, both as an off-campus and an on-campus issue. Editors are arming themselves with facts and getting concerned about what's happening to the earth's ecological balance. The U.S. Student Press Association's 1970 College Editors' Conference, which focused on ecology, was indicative of this new issue in the campus press.

Now that coverage—that concern—needs to be expanded if indifference and ignorance among readers is to be totally eliminated. The campus press must continue to supply expertise and inspiration to spark further the youth movement against destruction of our planet. Moreover, the student press can itself become a prime force in the environmental campaign.

The purpose of this chapter is to suggest how eco-activists can stimulate publicity, both on their own and by convincing editors to give their efforts support and attention in the campus and commercial media. I'm not going to belabor the fine points of PR; eco-activists should just use common sense and courtesy with newsmen, and try to think as they think.

The UNESCO conference at which Wolf Von Eckhardt attacked the press grabbed headlines not simply because of its environmental theme, but because of a youth takeover. An unsilent minority, mostly uninvited college students, made their presence felt by raising challenging issues early in the conference. That presence was publicized because it was a youth presence and because the current environment movement is essentially a youth movement. The problem, therefore, is not so much *getting* publicity, but *coping* with it, getting the most value from every effort and from every media. Hard sell Mad-Ave overkill is not necessary. If your group's goals and projects are legitimate, there should be no need to do things just to attract attention.

If you're just starting up and considering a name for your ecology action group, remember that editors like acronyms. There's nothing wrong with Ecology Action as a name, but GASP really grabs you, or so the Group Against Smelter Pollution at the University of Arizona thought. SCOPE, for Student Committee on Pollution in the Environment, is the name of the youth advisory group in the Federal Water Pollution Control Administration. You may want to avoid acronyms (considering the spate of them in the civil rights and anti-war movement) but newsmen are likely to use the first letters of the words in your group name anyway for brevity and to avoid repetition. So you might as well strive for something clever (but not embarrassing, like Foes of Pollution: FOP). Any creative, original, catchy name will grab the imagination of a headline writer. The University of Oregon deserves a prize for coming up with Nature's Conspiracy. A New York group has a winner with, simply, "SURVIVAL!" "Friends of the Earth" is also appropriate, and double-edged (FOE).

Now how about a statement of purpose, concise but comprehensive? Editors have to toss in some explanation of what QXZUP is when it makes news. Check out the goals of ENACT (Environmental Action for Survival) at the University of Michigan: "ENACT seeks to stimulate increasingly widespread awareness of the delicate balance upon which life depends, and of the rapidity with which man is destroying this vital balance. We will take action to halt this destruction. By providing accurate information and guidelines to effective action, we will work to encourage commitment, by individuals and by institutions, to attack these critical problems with a sense of urgency and priority." Such a statement is full of words media-men like to stress: *stimulate, awareness, vital, action, information, guidelines, commitment, attack, urgency, priority.*

In playing their game, remember that newsmen like to have somebody to peg as "leader" or "spokesman."

Even though your group may have no clear-cut leadership, someone will have to play leader; otherwise statements or actions might be attributed to the entire group or just any individual—not so cool, considering the diversity of the movement.

Fact sheets explaining your leadership structure (or non-structure) with people's home phone numbers and general background should be given to the press when you start up, and thereafter should be available at each activity. Any other material distributed publicly should also be available to the press.

Besides contacting commercial daily and weekly newspapers and broadcasters in your area, approach other publications—the monthly city magazine nearby, "shoppers," and newsletters of community groups and labor unions. Get together with your school's PR department or news bureau about a major feature for distribution statewide. The people there can be a big help if their heads are in the right place. Remember, they get paid for boosting the school's image, and may have to compromise if your group does something that might be considered a bad reflection on the institution. Other campus publications such as the alumni magazine, departmental publications and yearbook should also be encouraged to get into ecology. And if you're into something really unique or newsworthy, don't hesitate to contact national media. Get to know campus or area stringers for the major publications, and be sure to keep the local wire service guys posted. If you uncover some really gross environmental wrongdoing with national implications, contact such respected muckraking journals as *Hard Times, New Republic* or *The Nation*.

The campus radio station can help with spots, documentaries, and continuing coverage. The station can carry speeches and seminar sessions live for the whole campus to hear. Or, if you want to try something really far-out, how about developing for radio a futuristic *War of the Worlds* type forecast of environmental destruction?

Don't overlook unusual ways of getting the message out. Buttons are a medium. Art classes can design and print posters and handbills unique enough to stand out on overloaded bulletin boards. Advertising classes can do public service ads to offer the local press. (All media run public service ads, why not something about the environment?) A broadcasting class can prepare spots for radio and TV stations; copywriting classes can help with copy. Drama students can spark street theater. The campus bookstore can establish an ecology section.

Meanwhile, you should be busy starting your own paper or magazine (it should be unconventional if not underground) and tooling up a speakers bureau. Run a "dirty pictures" contest for the best photos, drawings, and sculpture depicting our dirtied environment. A multi-media exhibit in the union or some other semi-public place will draw attention. For their "Urban Futures USA" conference, Rice University students set up scaffolding, stoplights, flashers, junked cars, gas pumps, signs and other manifestations of the urban reality that soon became the talk of the campus. Field trips can become meaningful "on-site" press conferences.

Though the medium may be the message, the event itself is a very crucial part of what's transmitted. So strive for far-out symbolic actions on meaningful, relevant issues that will seize the imagination and commitment of the press and the public. The overall rule of thumb is to localize the greater issues at hand in the ecology movement. Don't just demonstrate against water pollution; pick a nearby polluted stream and wage a cleanup campaign. Everybody knows industry kills; identify *which* industries. Shine a giant searchlight on belching smokestacks at night. Give DIS-honor awards to polluters. Picket. Have a mock funeral for an internal combustion engine. A simple idea can blossom into a great publicity-getter, and accomplish something in its own right. Pete Seeger set out last summer with songs and a sailing sloop on the befouled Hudson River and turned on thousands to the problem of water pollution.

What about militancy? Violence is certainly dramatic, and it certainly makes news. But too often the message is lost in this medium. Editors and the public lose sight of *why* something is done and get caught up in *how*. They often don't understand that the central problem may really be more violent itself than the particular solution. In a moment of quasi-satirical despair, Norman Mailer suggested that citizens would have to "get muskets" and "explode all the factories." But before resorting to that extreme, or any action approximating it, eco-activists should exhaust all other possible ways to stop environmental destruction. Level-headed, reasonable, and honest action will win out in the end. After all, what we're after is ecological sanity. If people get turned off at what they consider our "insanity," our efforts may have diminishing returns.

There are situations, of course, that may demand action beyond lawful tactics. Eco-activists at the University of Texas, for example, climbed into trees that the school was determined to cut down. They had to be dragged down by police, at the orders of the regents. George Washington University and Georgetown University students camped out on the Three Sisters Islands threatened by construction of a new bridge across the Potomac River. They, too, were busted. Such illegal but non-violent tactics can dramatize an issue and generate support among students and community residents who otherwise would not become involved. In such cases a viable PR mechanism is especially necessary to make sure the media has all the facts and reports what's behind the militant actions and arrests. Moreover, growing militancy will serve as an indication of what might lie ahead. If young people who use peaceful tactics become frustrated because they see no hope from working within the system, escalated, illegal activities and even an ecological revolt may result.

Before long, journalists will play a bigger role in saving the earth than they now do as mere observers and reporters. If they are to serve their profession and their fellow men, journalists will become advocates for the ecological cause. They will serve their profession because the news media is in trouble. For once I find myself agreeing, but for different reasons, with Spiro Agnew. The media *has* grown "fat and irresponsible." There are "effete, impudent snobs" in our midst, but they are the media barons. The press today is *in*-credible. Because of its insistence on *objectivity,* the press is impotent. This objectivity, the distinguished David Deitch of the Boston *Globe* wrote in *The Nation,* "is pernicious to society as well as to the institutions of journalism. There is no evidence that it serves a public interest."

With an occasional "news analysis" the exception, journalism students are expected to bow down to the God of Objectivity. This may sound heretical, but what I'm advocating is advocacy journalism. It means, simply, "Get involved."

Advocacy journalism destroys the dangerous anonymity afforded by objectivity or "balance." A reporter then must be honest with his readers and must reveal his own biases. He can no longer evade personal responsibility for his work. Advocacy, openly admitted, requires an exposure of self, a willingness to undergo scrutiny, and, importantly, a commitment to excellence that is very demanding. When a reporter knows his beat he should be expected to write what's on his mind. Deitch points out the absurdity of a veteran statehouse reporter who never gave his readers the benefit of his own opinion on state politics or a contract kickback.

Of course, talking about this is not going to make it happen. What will make it happen is a radical transformation of the American newspaper into a social participant, not a mere observer. Reporters and editors must become willing to get off the fence.

Campus newspapers can advocate sane environmental policies and practices in a number of ways. Besides regular ongoing coverage of this new "beat," student papers should run articles by local ecologists and undertake special investigations on their own. The *Daily Student* at the University of Indiana probed regional campus growth in a feature series, and Rensselaer Polytechnic Institute's paper took a hard look at the new campus plan. The *Daily Emerald* at the University of Oregon devoted an entire edition of its *Salt* to the environment, with exciting graphics, too. The underground *Argus* at the University of Michigan also did a special, with an ecological "Declaration of Interdependence" on the cover. A number of student papers already use the apocalyptic cartoons of Ron Cobb. Sawyer Press in Los Angeles, which syndicates Cobb's excellent pictorial parables, has cooperated with organizations wishing to illustrate posters. (The U.S. Student Press Association blew up the great "Progress in America the Beautiful" cartoon on a poster for the College Editors Conference on ecology.) Other papers reprint Pat Oliphant's drawings, a number of which are related to the environment. Besides using College Press Service and Liberation News Service articles on the environment, papers can subscribe to *earth readout* (ERO), a new ecological news service of sorts. But true advocacy may entail more than mere use of a pen. Student journalists may have to man the barricades if no one else on campus moves.

Allen Ginsberg has written:

> For the world is a mountain of shit. If it's going to be moved at all, it's got to be taken by handfuls.

What advocate journalists do is the dirty work. They get off the fence and take a handful. At the meeting of the U.S. Student Press Association in Boulder, just before Woodstock, student editors began realizing the necessity of politicizing their papers. Ken Kelley, who quit the Michigan *Daily* to start the Ann Arbor *Argus,* left the USSPA editors with these words: "Either you join us now, brothers and sisters, or we'll all be smashed by honky power pigs. Like Eldridge Cleaver said, 'Either you're part of the solution, or you're part of the problem.' "

The Statement of Purpose: Two Models

We of ECOS believe that a crisis exists which endangers the future of America, of mankind, and of life itself. We believe that all of us as human beings share the responsibility for this crisis.

We hold that these are the root causes:

—an exploding population, which consumes vast and ever-increasing quantities of the entire world's energy and material resources, with little thought of the consequences . . .

—an aggressive technology and economic system, which, in a rush to provide for and to profit from the human population, destroys other forms of life and contaminates our environment to a degree unprecedented in human history . . .

—a burgeoning military establishment equipped with and committed to employ from its arsenal both nuclear and biochemical weapons in defense of this system . . .

—a set of traditional values which may have sustained the human species in the past but which have led instead to the above problems and now inhibit us from responding to the present crisis.

Against this dark picture is the individual man or woman, increasingly alienated from others and impotent to act, confronted by large, unresponsive institutions and the collapse of meaningful, humane communities.

We believe that this crisis will not be resolved solely by traditional conservation activities, obstructionist tactics, force of arms, unilateral government action, or independent or uncoordinated efforts; nor will the solution be found in new scientific discoveries or technological advances within the present system.

We propose to create a fresh ethical response to our environment; a self-sustaining way of life in which man views himself as part of and as dependent upon the natural ecosystem. ECOS is a starting point.

We reject as unacceptable:

—a world in which unlimited population growth and unlimited economic expansion are accepted uncritically as beneficial . . .

—a world in which any person lives in luxury and privilege while many others live in hunger or oppression . . .

—a world in which men and women view themselves as separated from the earth and the inspirations of nature . . .

—a world in which the individual is victimized by the impersonal machinery of his technology . . .

—a world in which people turn to violence, anarchy, or totalitarianism to resolve their dissatisfaction with government, technology, or society.

In coming together to meet these problems we understand that the greatest enemy of mankind at present is man, and that our source of hope in averting this environmental/social/ecological crisis rests with the community of concern and action which we are building together.

We see at least three tasks before us:

—making the human population at large, and its political leaders in particular, aware of the crisis and the fact that it *does* affect them . . .

—undertaking constructive campaigns to halt or, at least, delay the excessive growth of our population, the depletion of our resources, and the pollution of our water, earth, and air . . .

—developing basic alternatives to our present way of life and view of the world which will be more functional, more adaptive, and more stable in the future.

The time for decision and action is now. The responsibility cannot be left for future generations—we may be the last generation able to choose an effective course of action.

*   *   *

The only *natural resource* left on this planet that man seems unable to reduce to the disaster level is the capacity for discontent. Our organization, *Environment!,* is designed to harvest this resource and apply it to the complex problems of survival.

After generations of hibernation the power of *focused action* has awakened America. In our time we see man shaking free of his lethargy, his apathy, and demanding something more than mere minimums. The people of our time want a universally better life, and freedom from the tyranny of poverty. Our people want each man to have the opportunity of being a man, each woman a woman and each child an adult. At the root of all these problems, and basic to the ills of all societies, we believe, is the rapid deterioration of our environment.

Young people today just entering into their adult years have been scarred by war, and strengthened by it. We are not speaking of the war in Viet Nam, of Biafra or the Middle East, but of the war at home. A generation of Americans now leaving their teen-age years and early twenties behind them are the shock troops of what can be the new kind of man—the man who belongs to more than himself and is responsible to more than his own pleasures.

There are already close to 360 conservation-oriented organizations in the Greater New York area alone and, nationally, there are thousands. *Environment!* can function as a unique organization, however, as a service corps to these smaller groups by mobilizing support for their projects. Our resource, and our strength, is manpower. Tens, even hundreds of thousands of young people are ready to participate in the battle for a clean world, to pay the bill for generations of neglect, indifference, abuse. They are willing because they are aware. They are aware because they have looked around them and seen their world and seen that it is not good. And they have learned from their times that what is not good can be changed.

We are a positive organization. We are not in opposition to anything except the further corruption of our environment and the environment of our children. We are *for* clean, breathable air, we are *for* clean water, we are *for* urban planning, we are *for* a healthy environment, *for* the preservation of the living laboratories of wild places, *for* the continued existence of wildlife, *for* a better life for man and animal alike. We take these things, a clean and healthy environment aesthetically enriched by wildlife and natural wonders, as the inalienable rights of all future generations of mankind. We are prepared to muster the energies of the New American and create for the first time on Earth a responsible custodianship over that which has been left to us. We accept our environment in far worse shape than it has ever been in the past; we shall leave it to our descendents in far better shape than it has been in for several generations.

Without qualification, *Environment!* is against the war in Viet Nam, against all war and against all forces that would deny any human being his dignity and his right to a full, rich life according to his own standards. However, after years of political activity and anti-war activity we are sophisticated enough to know that Viet Nam, civil rights, Biafra and all of the other apparently consuming problems of our time will be academic if the environments of our planet lose their integrity and their power to support the lives of men. We feel that the loss of that power is a very real danger. We intend to fight, in a positive way as an action corps, to preserve what is left and recapture as much as possible of what has been taken away.

PART VII

rapping it out

"Resolving in essence the quest of human survival and the quality of human life on a planet of fragile hospitality—this is an issue which must become of immediate concern to all segments of society."

Blueprint for a Teach-In

Long before plans began to materialize for a National Environment Teach-In in the spring of 1970, student activists at the University of Michigan at Ann Arbor were already planning to do their own thing a month earlier. The Michigan Teach-In thus became the prototype for Earth Day activities throughout the nation. And behind the action in Ann Arbor was—and is—a group called ENACT (Environmental Action for Survival Committee). Here are the guidelines members of ENACT drafted for their teach-in:

A teach-in is an extra-curricular effort to reach across the limitations of professional and departmental barriers to inform and to provide opportunities for action. The extraordinary nature of a teach-in can capture and focus the attention of the entire community on specific issues for intensive study, discussion and action. Expert, but diverse, opinions are widely disseminated through formal presentations, panel discussions and workshops. Emphasis is upon individual understanding and involvement.

The result, for many participants, is an informed awareness of the issues, realization of common purpose and a commitment to organized and persistent action.

The teach-in is a newsworthy event; effective publicity

can carry this message to a far greater audience in the community and beyond, than would an equivalent effort invested in seminars and public meetings spread over a longer time interval.

Issues of environmental quality and survival are particularly suitable for the teach-in medium. These are issues in which the general populace must take an interest, and make a new commitment to action, if the problems are to be solved through orderly change. Teach-ins on the environment offer an unusual opportunity to involve a broad spectrum of the community—particularly students—in this enormous challenge.

Michigan's Teach-In on the Environment

Coordinated through the ENACT Steering Committee, a number of working committees are preparing the detailed plans for all aspects of the Teach-In. The total effort will involve three phases: (1) the Teach-In Itself, (2) the Momentum Effort, and (3) the Follow-Through.

The teach-in itself

Events during the four-day Teach-In period will be centered on the university campus, in the local schools and in the general regional community. Some of these events will be occurring simultaneously, others will seek to enlist joint participation from all sectors.

On campus, ENACT will sponsor a structured program of events. Simultaneously, individual departments, schools and organizations will hold in-house and specialized programs coordinated in the over all events program.

The Teach-In will begin on Wednesday evening with a major kick-off event held in the 14,000 seat Events Building. This program will combine mixed-media presentations, environmentally-oriented entertainment by nationally prominent folk singers and a rock band, and two addresses: one by a leader among environmental politicians, the other a leading policy-oriented ecologist. It is hoped that this program can be held with no admission charge.

Thursday will be emphasized as a day of events in the local schools. A community rally will be held Thursday evening. Radio and television will be used for special programming in conjunction with the Teach-In, including a "Town Meeting of the Air" on environmental issues. On campus, there will be in-house events in departments, and films and other exhibits will be emphasized. In-house programs in departments will continue during Friday but the focus will return to centralized programming, with a series of major speakers during the afternoon. The general topic of these presentations will be kinds of environmental problems and appropriate solutions. During the evening a major panel presentation will deal with problem definition, focusing on a determination of underlying causes. The panel will be followed by a discussion period and by workshops and informal talks with panel participants.

Saturday will conclude action programs in the community ("instant" construction of a vest-pocket park, petition canvassing, etc.). Arrangements may be made for a legislative hearing to be held in Ann Arbor that morning, dealing with environmental problems. During the afternoon the focus will be upon varieties of roles in change: citizen, government official, specialist, student, etc. Workshops will be held during the later afternoon following up these topics.

The program will conclude on Saturday evening with a major address on the environment and man's future, a synthesizing discussion of the issue and the potential for solving our environmental problems.

Action projects, literature distribution, and publicity events will occur throughout the Teach-In period. An Ecology House will be open on campus at all times for exhibits, music, and informal discussions.

Off-campus, a coordinated schedule of events will be conducted in the local elementary and high schools.

These events will be largely student-planned and administered, although ENACT will provide major speakers, films and exhibits. Teachers at all levels will be provided with special teaching materials for the period, highlighting many aspects of environmental issues. Teachers' workshops may be held in advance.

A schedule of major assemblies will be arranged to permit multiple appearances by a major speaker particularly attractive to young people. This will serve to keynote the high school events.

All media will be used to seek involvement by community groups and individuals. Service clubs and other groups will be encouraged to plan special events during the week to deal with environmental problems. Programs, exhibits, speakers and workshops on local problems will be scheduled in coordination with existing groups spearheading these efforts. An environmental fair will run continuously during the Teach-In period.

Religious groups will be encouraged to give attention to environmental matters in sermons, Sunday schools, adult meetings and bulletins.

Legislative and executive declaration of the Teach-In week as "Improve Michigan's Environment Week" will be sought at the state level, with parallel designations in local jurisdictions.

The momentum effort

A fundamental part of the organizational and planning work building up to the Teach-In itself will be a staged momentum effort:

> • *University seminars and workshops on man and the environment.* A weekly series of these seminars will be led by both university faculty and guest lecturers, representing fields such as natural science, social sciences, engineering and design. Workshops organized by faculty and students will follow each seminar.

• *Regional school systems.* Speakers will be provided for all elementary and secondary schools for talks both during regular classes and in extra-curricular sessions. A block of night school classes on environmental matters may be scheduled. Educational programs will also be coordinated with nearby universities and junior and community colleges.

• *Community seminars.* Weekly seminars of special interest to the community, focusing especially on local issues, are being scheduled. Community organizations will be informed of the availability of speakers on environmental issues.

• *Speakers bureau.* ENACT will serve as a registration center for the many graduate students, faculty, and citizens who have indicated a willingness to serve in the momentum effort programs.

• *Departmental speakers.* Many outstanding speakers are brought to campus each semester through funds available to individual departments of schools. Through Teach-In committees established in each school, unconventional speakers, or speakers of interest to large segments of the university will be recommended. ENACT will provide more widespread publicity than is normally given such talks.

• *Major speakers.* During the month prior to the Teach-In itself, one or two major speakers will be scheduled for campus-wide talks under sponsorship of ENACT. Provocative speakers will be sought to assure publicity impact.

• *Information files.* Extensive monitoring of journals, magazines, books and newspapers for information on specific environmental issues has begun. This information will be indexed and made available to anyone. In addition, a newsletter with information on pertinent issues is being published regularly.

• *General publicity.* Reading lists are already in circulation. Displays will be set up in local bookstores, the public libraries and elsewhere. Full use of all media is planned.

• *Action projects.* These will be undertaken during all phases: momentum, the Teach-In itself, and follow-through. Appropriate action projects, from many presented, are being considered by several groups within the Steering Committee as well as by Teach-In committees at the school or department level. The projects may include:

—*Participatory actions.* Organization of groups to undertake a specific project, such as cleaning an area of litter, aid in identifying violators of pollution regulations, design and implementation of a park area, etc. Emphasis will be placed on interdisciplinary efforts and joint community-university projects.

—*Demonstrations.* Events intended to draw attention to particular problems are planned.

—*Legislation.* Specific legislation at the state level will be selected (or drafted) for promotion and publicity. If possible, legislative hearings will be scheduled in Ann Arbor during the momentum effort.

—*Litigation.* ENACT may bring suit to enjoin some prominent environmental abuse, in order to create public awareness of the law as an effective instrument for environmental action.

The Teach-In itself will culminate a growing momentum of interest and concern. It will focus this concern constructively and it will create a wide demand for continuing action programs. The follow-through from the Teach-In is planned to include the following:

Major events of the Teach-In and results of action projects will be publicized at the local, state and national level as a demonstration of a constructive, broadly based attack on problems of the human environment:

Publication of major addresses, panel discussions and guidelines in pocketbook format for rapid and widespread distribution;

Production of videotapes and tape-recordings for use in other schools and on radio and television.

Many on-going action projects and educational programs will be initiated during the momentum effort and the Teach-In itself. Continuation of these projects will be a major function of ENACT.

A major follow-through effort of ENACT will be to maintain interdisciplinary and university-community channels opened by Teach-In events.

As a permanent campus and community organization, ENACT will continue to carry out its stated goals, evolving its procedures, modes of action, and specific projects according to the circumstances. The Teach-In itself will have a major impact on guiding the future work of ENACT to meet identified needs and styles of this campus and community.

Conclusion

The basic planning philosophy for all activities affiliated with the Teach-In—before, during, after—is to contribute to the building of informed and action-oriented public concern for the human environment. This subject matter, effectively programmed in the Teach-In and follow-through activities, is an ideal vehicle to open communications between campuses and the general citizenry. Resolving in essence the question of human survival and the quality of human life on a planet of fragile hospitality—this is an issue which must become of immediate concern to all sectors of society. Only in this way will effective action be motivated through the numerous channels—economic, political, and social—

which contribute to environmental misuse, and which are the necessary means to environmental improvement and protection.

The University of Michigan 1970 Teach-In on the Environment, culminating a staged effort to inform and mobilize concern, can focus public attention on constructive action. Its planned follow-through can broaden and deepen the impact, carrying this urgent issue of environmental quality, with all of its implications for human life, far closer to the concerns and self-interests of all whom it touches.

by Lee Horstmann

Tips on Conducting
Environmental Conferences

Are you really interested in getting together with some other people to search for ways to improve the environment? Do *not* hire four super-experts to discuss for three days "Man vs. the Sea" with one large, hastily-convened group. Your project is likely to be far more concretely creative by bringing in four younger professionals to discuss for a week "Flotation Systems for Ocean Cities" with several small subgroups of participants, all of whom are well-grounded in the problems and who have let you know what their questions are.

Noted authorities generally overcharge and under-think for student seminars. It is far better (and cheaper) to look carefully for well-recommended younger scholars and junior authorities. Big names can invoke initial interest in a conference and often lend respectability and legitimacy that otherwise might be lacking, but don't invite a Biggie for these reasons alone. The best source of information and ideas at the Rice conference was often the student delegates themselves.

Make your topic specific, after a long research period. Do you think you can build a study group around urban transportation? Okay. Study the situation yourself a

---

Lee Horstmann is president of the student government at Rice University.

while. Send short questionnaires to lots of specialists. You may discover that this subject boils down to a core issue, as many do (e.g., air pollution = internal combustion engines)—perhaps in this case the economic feasibility of automated highway systems. Our subject —the future of city living—was, although popular, far too broad for really fruitful discussion. We should have narrowed the topic down to any one of several key issues: automation, overpopulation, information and sensory overload, social mobility, or community breakdowns. For this reason, as well as the need to raise financial and/or academic endorsement for your project, count on at least one year of planning.

For funding, campus groups or private corporations in the area can be hit up. The school may kick in some money if sessions are open to all members of the campus community.

The shorter the study period is, the smaller the groups should be. For productive collaboration, people must get to feeling at ease with their colleagues, and alert to their analytical biases. We divided the 100 out-of-state delegates to URBAN FUTURES USA into 12-person groups, which were too large for a three-day meeting. As a result, there was a lot of stuffiness and circular talk. Strive for informality; give the groups freedom to determine their own direction.

Prepare the participants in advance. Before your study group ever comes together, circulate some relevant article reprints and a suggested reading list.

Demand feedback. If it shows that many are confused about issue X and bored to death by issue Z, gear your lecture sessions accordingly. At Rice, when we found that the delegates were most concerned about combating racism and political inertia, and were in greatest consensus about the need for decentralized cities, it was too late to exchange some of our urban planning specialists for some more psychiatrists and civic leaders. Also, it might be wise to convene your resource people a few days before the seminar begins.

Utilize talented professors (and administrators) on

your campus. Those local students who express a big
interest in the conference topic can help with arrangements. The masses of local students should not be over-
looked. Invite a limited number (perhaps based on
professors' recommendations) as delegates and make
general sessions campus-wide. At Rice, the campus
radio station broadcast major sessions live. A big factor
in stirring student interest was a far-out but meaningful
McLuhanesque exhibit on the urban landscape.

Consider wrapping up the conference with some form
of action, perhaps a resolution expressing the sense of
the study group about the problem under consideration
or some other overt demonstration to underscore the
significance of what has happened at the conference.

Finally, prepare an evaluation of what happened so
that future conference coordinators can gain from your
mistakes and successes. A conference report, with
verbatim major presentations and summaries of group
discussions, should be mailed to participants and other
interested parties.

by Connie Flateboe

The Student Environmental Congress: A Report from Stanford

The campus movement to involve students in environmental quality issues gained substantial momentum in the fall of 1969 during a Student Environmental Congress at Stanford University. In effect, the Congress was intended to provide a platform for concerned students to discuss ways in which they could work to halt the population explosion and reverse the accelerating rate of environmental deterioration. It was important that participants come prepared to present ideas rather than sit passively, as is the style of most conferences. And prepared they came. The reports from key Congress committees attests to that.

The *Committee on Undergraduate Curricula* agreed that "traditional habits of higher education are not embraced by the present generation of students, especially as the philosophy and structure of higher education relates to the generation's confrontation with worldwide environmental deterioration. The system has a built-in lag time; it assumes that a freshman will not make a positive contribution to society for at least four to even ten years after entering college. Our society's problems are too urgent and *we can't wait that long*. We want to contribute now; we want to see a payoff from our efforts. Rather than study subjects and situations

Connie Flateboe is the Sierra Club's campus representative.

at a high level of abstraction, we are searching for mechanisms of interfacing our educational system with society at large. We want to direct student energies toward problems within their social context. We want to merge our roles of student and citizen. The Environmental Crisis is the problem; we must all address ourselves to its solution."

The committee considered environmental programs as "tools for innovation in college curricula. Nontraditional problems require non-traditional educational solutions. We cannot expect professors to invent ready-made courses and curricula to solve our educational problems. In many cases schools do not have financial or intellectual resources for new formal programs. We therefore emphasize the concepts of participatory education, such as learning groups and do-it-yourself research. Many needs exist, according to the type of institution. In junior colleges, emphasis is on general education courses, and those courses should be required to emphasize strongly environmental problems. University groups, with greater resources at hand, will tend to emphasize student research on the technical aspect of environmental problems. We all want to turn out graduates who will be change agents for our society. To that end, we urge students now to constitute themselves as change agents in existing curricula: to search for, campaign for, institute, and to the extent possible, to execute environmental study programs for all the colleges. If satisfactory programs can't be worked out within existing departmental structures, the interdisciplinary, extramurally-funded programs should be attempted. Find resource people, materials and equipment, and *do it*.

"The primary educational goal of every student should be awareness of existing and potential problems. We seek an environmental conscience, and a sense of social responsibility, accompanied by enlightened activism; that is to say, a direct participation in environmental control functions of government, industry and academia. To this end, we desire to make of the college a milieu which will pose problems and offer opportunities for students to discover special interests, career opportunities, and self-discipline through actual participation in professional-type activism."

Specific guidelines from the committee to student environmental groups:

1) Get students appointed to and to appear before educational planning councils; advocate establishment of environmental programs and recruitment of professional staff. In all cases, urge establishment of general education courses in environmental problems for non-specialists. The public must be educated; let's begin with ourselves.

2) Encourage "relevant" attitudes in specialized courses; e.g., propose to analyze local surface waters in analytical chemistry lab. The growing importance of environment could be discussed in many academic contexts—political, aesthetic, even rhetorical.

3) Stimulate public and classroom exposure to controversy through sponsorship of teach-ins and professorial debates. Advocate joint teaching of classes by professors from many disciplines.

4) Form study groups to look into environmental problems of local interest. Seek support and encouragement of local industries and governmental agencies; join with and help establish local citizen action groups.

5) Urge academic recognition and promotion of professors for problem-solving activities and for leadership functions, in addition to the present emphasis on "scholarly" research.

The *Environmental Bill of Rights Committee* submitted the following resolution:

That among the rights retained under the Ninth Amendment of the Constitution of the United States are the rights of present and future generations to the enjoyment, maintenance and restoration of such environmental quality so as to promote the general health and/or welfare and assure optimal conditions for life.

Such rights do include the rights to clean air, pure water, pure food, freedom from overpopulation and from excessive and unnecessary noise.

The *Committee for Legislative Proposals* urged that the following measures be adopted through appropriate legislation:

• Establishment of a (California) State Environmental Quality Agency which would bring an integrated, ecosystem approach to the environmental aspects of state policy decisions. Such an agency would be appointive, and its representation broad both in terms of interests represented and professional expertise. This agency would be given a veto power over projects that do not conform with long-range state environmental interests.

• Levy of a tax on automobiles at the time of sale, based on the amount of effluents produced by that automobile. For autos using the internal combustion engine (what else?) this tax would be correspondingly high, thus creating a strong marketplace incentive for the development of low-emission autos such as those powered by steam or gas turbines. This tax measure could also be coupled with the eventual banning of internal combustion engines altogether.

• New taxes on the sale of leaded gasoline to encourage the development of substitutes for the lead additive, with its severely polluting effects.

• Creation by the California state government of a coastline commission along the lines of the

San Francisco Bay Conservation and Development
Commission, which would have full powers to
regulate such matters as beach access, development
and use of the coastline.

• Legalization of all forms of birth control, including abortion, as a basic human right. The
federal and state tax structure should be revised
to discourage rather than encourage any increase in
dependents; the government should pursue an
active information campaign for the "prevention
of unwanted children"; the provision in the California Health and Safety Code requiring all birth
control devices to be sold only through pharma-
cists should be eliminated.

The *Committee on Public Education* dealt with the
problem of how to increase environmental awareness
through the mass media. Newspaper pages and the air-
waves are among the most effective means of reaching
people. By creating news, campus and conservation
groups can also create this necessary awareness.

Individual students may participate in the public
educational process in a number of ways: by producing
a weekly column on ecological problems in the campus
paper, as guests or callers on radio and TV talk shows,
by writing letters to the editors of campus and community newspapers, and by securing coverage of the
campus group's activities in the special feature sections
of local newspapers.

"Advertising," the committee pointed out, "should
also be used for access to the media. Newspapers and
television frequently participate in public service campaigns. TV stations are particularly anxious to oblige
when their license renewals are approaching and they
need to prove their worth to the community. Radio
stations frequently broadcast public service spot announcements free."

The technical skills found in college film and journalism departments should be tapped to produce docu-

mentaries and commercials; professors should be encouraged to suggest environmental issues as subjects for class projects.

Once campus groups develop good relationships with news media on campus and in the community, they must provide a reliable body of facts about ecological problems, and make suggestions as to what people can do once they are aware of those problems.

The *Committee on University Research on the Environment* presented the following recommendations:

The newly-formed Student Environmental Confederation (SEC) should promptly devise a faculty questionnaire requesting a short statement on environmental research studies in progress. Members should circulate this among all faculty at their respective campuses, assemble a directory of research for the campus, and forward a summary to the statewide organization (SEC) for incorporation into a California directory of environmental research.

On their own initiative, or through regional coalitions, campus environmental groups should request from appropriate state and federal agencies lists and abstractions of all funded research in their area pertaining to environmental problems. Responses shall be added to the local and statewide directories as rapidly as practical.

Central to the movement on California campuses to get students involved in finding solutions to environmental problems was the Congress' *Committee on a Statewide Student Organization.* The idea for a student environmental coordinating organization and the basic constitution for it were formulated in 1967 by students from Active Conservation Tactics at the University of California at Berkeley and Davis. The organization created at that time was called the National Campus Coordinating Council. The NCCC carried on for a time coordinating the relatively few campus conservation groups in the country, but it soon expired for lack of sufficient national interest on campus, no money, and no regular staff to keep the organization alive. The Stanford Conservation Group revived the NCCC constitution for the Student Congress, then turned it over to the SEC.

The goal of the SEC in California is "to provide an effective and continuing coordinating structure of state-wide scope in working for the environment and for appreciation of scenic, historic, open space, wilderness, outdoor, and urban recreational resources, and for the protection of total environmental quality, through a program of coordinated action and education." As of January, 1970, twenty college and high school campus ecology groups belonged to SEC, with membership reaching from Humboldt State College to the University of San Diego.

by Connie Flateboe

The UNESCO Manifesto

The week following the Student Environmental Congress at Stanford, students from across the nation converged on San Francisco to attend the 13th Annual Conference of the U.S. National Commission on UNESCO. The "youth delegates" had done their homework, and their recommendations at this conference soon reflected their impatience to get on with specific solutions.

Youth delegates rejected the premise that the salvation of mankind depends on the control of land, air and sea. They found instead that man depends on the control of *man,* and that "life's pursuits can be predicated on equality, dignity, peace, beauty, and compassion for man and nature."

On a national scale, the delegates urged:

• The mobilization of a national effort to attain stability of numbers and equilibrium between man and nature—*by a specified date.*

• The immediate assumption of a massive, federally-financed study to determine the optimum carrying capacity of our country, on the community, city, county, state and national levels, with this carrying capacity to be predicated on the quality of life, the impact upon world resources, and the tolerance of natural systems.

• The adoption of new measures of national well-being, incorporating indices other than the rate of growth of the GNP, the consumption of energy resources, and international credit rating.

• The immediate rejection of international economic competition as valid grounds for the direction of national policy.

On an international scale, the delegates endorsed:

• A proposal that the leaders of all nations through the United Nations General Assembly declare that a state of environmental emergency exists on the planet earth.

• The creation of colleges of human ecology and survival sciences on campuses in the member nations of the United Nations.

• The creation of national and global plans for the determination of optimum population levels and human distribution patterns.

• The creation of national and world-wide commissions on environmental deterioration and rehabilitation.

• A proposal that the United Nations General Assembly adopt a covenant of ecological rights similar to the U.N. covenant of human rights.

Politically, delegates pledged to work actively for change by all available methods, including:

• Sending lobbyists to local, state and national capitals to speak personally to elected officials.

• Drawing up specific proposals to be offered to competing candidates in primary or general elections.

- Supporting officials who have taken a strong stand for a healthy environment and working for their reelection.

- Campaigning for the defeat of candidates whose positions don't make ecological sense.

- Boycotting industries that disregard ecological sense by irresponsibly polluting the environment.

The youth delegates also circulated petitions addressed to President Nixon, the texts of which are reprinted here:

"We, having concluded that the species Homo Sapiens is in a crisis situation, ask the United Nations and President Nixon to declare a state of international environmental emergency.

"Due to the environmental deterioration of the Earth, a National Emergency should be declared. As such, the following is recommended:

1. Supersonic Transport (SST):

a) We demand the immediate termination of the SST project, with its funds applied to urban mass transport systems.

b) No U.S. carrier shall be allowed to fly any SST.

c) No SST of any airline, domestic or foreign, shall pass through the air space of the United States.

d) No airline with SST service shall book any flight through U.S. travel services.

2. Population Stabilization:

In order to stabilize the population, the federal government must subsidize and support all birth control methods:

a) Free sterilization.

b) Available contraceptive practices.

c) Free elective abortion.

In addition, the government should restructure the tax through financial incentives for families with no more than two children, discontinue the present policy of dependency deductions for minor children.

3. Pesticides:

We must ban production, importation, exportation and use in the United States of persistent pesticides such as DDT, except in cases of emergency, under strict controls.

4. Packaging:

All non-biodegradable, non-returnable packing materials, wrappings and containers must be removed from production.

PART VIII

a capitol colloquy

MOGILL: I just want to point out to Congress that it seems to be ignoring the problems of the cities these days, and that can't go on, because if it does, you know the consequences as well as I do.

McCLOSKEY: It is the American public that chooses its representation. And ten-to-one, in the city you speak of that is going down the drain, there is a Congressman who gives no attention to the environment. . . .

A Capitol Colloquy

To most young people—and especially to those who are deeply concerned about the quality of the environment—U.S. Senators and Congressmen must seem remote figures indeed. One can read about them in the newspaper, occasionally see them on television and, whenever pending legislation demands it, write them a letter. But few young people have the opportunity to engage their U.S. legislators in a direct and meaningful dialogue.

Such an opportunity was provided in the preparation of this handbook. At the request of the editors, Michael Kitzmiller, legislative assistant to Rep. Richard Ottinger (D.-N.Y.); Nancy Mathews, an Ottinger aide assigned to assist Earth Day teach-in groups, and Robert Waldrop, the Sierra Club's assistant Washington representative, arranged a tape-recorded colloquy among three members of the U.S. Congress identified with environmental issues and seven spokesmen for the under-30 generation. The participants:

Senator Philip Hart (D.-Mich.)
Rep. Paul McCloskey (R.-Calif.)
Rep. Ottinger
Kenneth Mogill, University of Michigan law student

James Moorman of the Center for Law and Social
   Policy
Marie Nahikian, conference coordinator for the
   U.S. Student Press Association
Ron Peterson, Yale University law student
Bill Sievert, editor of The College Press Service
Skip Spensley, George Washington University law
   student
John Zeh, editor of *Moderator* Magazine

The colloquy opened with a lively discussion of the
plan to open the North Slope of Alaska to exploitation
of its petroleum resources.

JAMES MOORMAN: I'd like to know if the government
is going to sit by and let the petroleum industry destroy
Alaska?

PHILIP HART: If the tape records a pause, it means
that Congressman Ottinger and Senator Hart were flab-
bergasted. I would hope Congress would be intolerant of
the destruction of any of the 50 states. That's sort of a
bromide answer, so let's get more specific. Isn't the
question whether technology will permit the extraction
of oil without in fact destroying or damaging the land?
The safeguards have to be built in, heaven knows.

RON PETERSON: It seems to me that we should throw
into this equation whether or not we need that oil at all,
or whether we might forego the development of the oil
fields in hopes of someday developing the technology to
allow development in a way that's not going to destroy
the state. It shouldn't be the policy of Congress to allow
the complete destruction of the environment of the State
of Alaska to satisfy oil interests which may in fact support a good number of Congressmen, but may not in
fact reflect the interest of the public in this issue.

HART: But you're assuming that technology today
would not permit the safe extraction and transport of
oil, and I don't think we know that. Now, I acknowledge
that the temptation would be to short-circuit the safe-

guards, to do less than would be fair to Alaska because of the temptation to get cheaper oil, which, in fact, you could get. I don't say that we should permit that.

PETERSON: So, are you willing to forego development of the Alaskan oil fields if technology is not such that at a reasonable cost we could protect the environment? Wouldn't you be willing to leave Alaska undeveloped?

HART: You're asking which claim should have priority.

PETERSON: That's correct.

HART: Cheaper oil or a non-damaged Alaska. I think the honest answer would compel you to say, well, if it's simply a small smudge that doesn't kill a duck but offends an aesthetic, yes, we'd tolerate the small smudge, but . . .

RICHARD OTTINGER: Well, I think we should err on the side of preserving Alaska. But the question was what will we *do,* and I'm afraid we'll err on the side of risking Alaska for oil . . . Now, in my own experience, I've found that most of our progress—in protecting any environment—has been made in the courts. And, you know, the Storm King case stopped Con Edison from building a huge hydroelectric plant on the Hudson. And I was successful as both plaintiff and participant in a suit against the Penn-Central Railroad to stop it from dumping oil into the Hudson River. And we've been successful in a suit against the State of New York to prevent it and the Corps of Engineers from putting a six-lane commercial highway along the Hudson River. And I do think that we've had more success in the courts than we have in the legislatures, either state or Federal. And as I see it, this is going to be one of the main thrusts. In the courts.

MARIE NAHIKIAN: Secretary Hickel has posed the basic question of who should pay the cost of cleaning up the environment. Secretary Hickel said if you buy a hundred-dollar suit but the manufacturer of that suit has to clean up the environment, then you might have to pay $101, the extra dollar going toward the clean-up. So who should pay this cost? The consumer?

HART: Well, we kid ourselves if we think we can find a way of *not* paying for it. We may gild it in a variety of fashions, but the money comes ultimately from your pocket or mine.

OTTINGER: You're going to have the clean-up price on the products that you pay for. The government isn't going to raise all the money needed to clean up the environment. Even if it could, the money would still be yours and mine.

JOHN ZEH: But why should industry be allowed to make a profit out of polluting the environment? Or taking the oil out of Alaska, for example?

OTTINGER: Because it . . . You know, the question basically is unfair. The process of exploitation of resources is a part of the industrial process, and this is a by-product of it. So long as you're going to have a free enterprise system, part of the cost of doing business is going to be part of the cost of either polluting the environment or paying to clean it up. And I don't see anything obnoxious in requiring industry to pay, and, therefore, the consumer to pay that cost. I think that is a better solution than trying to have the government pick up the entire cost and have the people pay for it through taxes and through the bureaucracy that you would have to build up in order to supervise the job.

SKIP SPENSLEY: I have a question. What's this going to do to inflation? I mean, is it going to continue to increase it?

HART: Are we agreed you and I are going to pay for it in whatever fashion?

SPENSLEY: Ultimately, yes.

HART: Disguised or direct. I think the Congressman's point is, as far as we can go with it, that you have to have a combination of the assignment of the burden. But I think we kid ourselves if we hope somebody else is really going to pay for it. We pay for not letting children under 12 work in the mines. And nobody thinks that's inconsistent with the social philosophy.

SPENSLEY: But how is Congress going to motivate industry to start cleaning up its own mess?

OTTINGER: I think there's going to be tremendous public pressure on industry. I think that that is going to enable us to pass very tough laws with injunctive powers. It's going to enable us to pass laws permitting class actions by the citizens for the enforcement of these laws. I don't think that industry is going to do it in large part voluntarily, because very frequently the cost is prohibitive and the guy that does it first, if everybody doesn't have to do it, will be at a prohibitive competitive disadvantage. I'll say this. I think that the laws that have been passed so far have been primarily to protect polluters rather than the public. What we've done is to stretch out the time for compliance, like the Clean Air Act (which went through my committee) under which a polluter can avoid any kind of enforcement action for something like 17 years. We can't tolerate that in the future. I don't think students are going to tolerate it. I think they're going to expose it. The politicians who are just mouthing the glories of cleaning up the environment are going to be called to task.

HART: Consider what Congressman Ottinger did in the Airport Construction Bill. This looks inside us. This isn't criticizing the fellow in Poughkeepsie or Detroit who is commercially abusing the environment. This is a question to ourselves, the Federal government: "What are you doing with respect to your own expenditures to ensure that they do not abuse the environment?" And the Ottinger amendment (which I hope I can get added to the bill on the floor) requires that in the selection of airport sites it be mandatory on the Federal government that the preferred site, the selected site, be the one that best adjusts to the environment, that least damages the environment, or does no damage. I think we ought to broaden that with respect to Federal expenditures generally, make the same requirement of the Department of Transportation when we're talking about mass transportation construction efforts. We must make sure we ourselves practice what we're telling the other guy he should do.

KEN MOGILL: You said that Congressman Ottinger's

amendment to the Airport Facilities Expansion Act is a step in the right direction. I would agree. But it's only a step. There are other ways in which the Federal government subsidizes pollution of the total environment—the way in which it subsidizes children who go off and run auto manufacturing industries and gobble up resources. What other ways can the Federal government go about cleaning its own house or at least preventing its effluvia from dirtying everybody else's house?

HART: Only by conditioning any dollar we authorize to this test: "Are you going to use it to damage your environment?"

PETERSON: Well, it seems to me that this is limited. For example, in the airport area you're always operating within a situation of cost constraints. And preservation of the environment is a very expensive activity. And if you are going to say, "We're going to give you this much to construct an airport and you can use this much in the best way possible to conserve the environment," and if the amount of money you give them is not sufficient for any type of environmental conservation program, the best you can do within the cost constraints is not good enough. The other problem, I think, is an administrative problem in that everybody thinks that he's saving the environment. I know the Army Corps of Engineers. No one in the Corps thinks he's despoiling the environment. But you talk to some of the people on the lands to which they've gone to construct their flood-control projects and they'll tell you a quite different story.

HART: Let me say you do touch the ultimate question of whether we are going to provide enough money to ensure that every action we take shall be as pure as human hands can treat the environment. And the answer to that hangs on whether we continue to dump 70 cents out of a dollar into the Pentagon and not worry about how they use it, with respect to the environment. But to the extent that the dollars the Federal government spends—several hundred billions of dollars—to the extent that we condition the use of those dollars on a maximum protection of the environment, the Ottinger approach is, as I see it, the only way you can do it.

PETERSON: I'm not trying to condemn this. I mean, it's a great idea. But unless we get the money to do what the approach is intended to do, it's completely verbalistic and a political approach, if I may use that term. I think the war in Viet Nam is a very excellent example because the public, I think, has been fooled into believing that we're getting out of Viet Nam just as I'm afraid they're going to be fooled into believing we're doing something about conservation. And that's the same thing that industry is trying to do privately. They're trying to fool the American public into believing that they are going to take upon themselves the responsibility to clean up this country. And I agree with Congressman Ottinger that industry is not going to do this by itself. It's going to try to fool the public. But I don't want congressmen trying to do the same thing. And this is what I think they're trying to do.

OTTINGER: I agree. Absolutely. A hundred percent. Industry and many congressmen—I'll certainly read Senator Hart out of that—*will* attempt to give the illusion of doing something about the environment without the substance. Senator Hart's been one of the leaders trying to change our priorities nationally. And that certainly is what I consider my main mission in Congress: to devote the necessary funds to improving the quality of life in the United States, preventing people from going hungry and preventing continued deterioration of our urban areas where the majority of the population is now. And that's another problem. Population. I do think the government is going to have to take a more courageous stand and try to encourage families not to have more than two or three children or something like that, to help everybody to be able to survive, to change tax incentives so that it will be more economical for couples to have small families instead of large ones.

BILL SIEVERT: Presidential advisor Moynihan said that the country could stand to have another 100 million people, to get up past 300 million. He said the problem is that all the people want to live in the same place, like Southern California or New York City or in the other great metropolitan areas. Do you agree with this? And what specifically can government agencies do in order to stop the population explosion, the crowding?

OTTINGER: The government can only act as far as the public permits it to act. That's one of the limitations of a democracy. Dictatorships are the most efficient forms of government possible. The trouble is, you're never going to be sure you get the right dictator. So I think our system is the best there is. What we have to start out on is an educational program. And the other thing that we can do is intervene to help people not have unwanted children. The government ought to make information on birth control available to people, and to make the devices for birth control available, perhaps subsidize them, perhaps even give them free to those who can't afford them, just as we give food stamps—or will be giving, I hope, food stamps for free.

HART: The question of overpopulation has been posed very dramatically by the director of the Michigan Department of Natural Resources, Dr. Ralph A. Mac-Mullan. And he put it in this light: that with only 7 percent of the world's population now in this country, we consume just about 50 percent of the natural resources in the world. At the present rate we'll double our population in 65 years. I don't know where Moynihan's hundred million more by 2000 will put us, but Dr. MacMullan's arithmetic was that if we do double our population in 65 years, we will then, if we maintain our present standard of living, be consuming all of the world's natural resources. And he suggests that the world won't stand still for that, nor should we.

MOGILL: The government recently purported to ban DDT, but this was a lie, with the exception of slowing up its use. And the reported ban on biological warfare agents is also a lie, in that it involved a redefinition which shifted most of the biological agents into the permissible category of chemical agents. Now, as members of Congress, you gentlemen are able to exercise the influence of your office to make this known, and you could propose legislation to accomplish what the administration claims to have accomplished.

OTTINGER: With respect to biological warfare limitations, I objected to the exemption from them of defoliants and of tear gas, and the exclusion, as well, of what has been defined as chemical weapons that in fact embody biological agents that will cause illness. And you know our present difficulty in coping with this. We're still a minority. Our voice hasn't been heard effectively. I think it's our job and your job to outrage people, to make them aware of this problem.

MOGILL: But we're accused of being a bunch of crazy radicals.

OTTINGER: The crazy radicals changed the attitude of this country very substantially, on all kinds of issues. The issues, when they first come out, *are* considered radical. Then, as the information gets around that the weaponry we are using and the industrial processes are killing us and jeopardizing the lives of Americans and perhaps the entire balance of nature in the world, it comes home to the people. Attitudes do change. It's very important that there be an element in our society that is willing to risk being called radicals and being subjected to social pressures, that will lead the way and will say things that are unpopular, and risk the reaction that comes from being unpopular in order to get these ideas forward and out to society where they can become acceptable.

SPENSLEY: As long as the students aren't congressmen.

OTTINGER: No. I spoke out against the Viet Nam war in the face of a poll in our district that showed 80 percent of the voters disagreed with me. And both Senator Hart and Pete McCloskey have taken similar courageous stands. So that isn't the case. But in order to be able to get a majority of Congress behind an issue, the issue just has to become more acceptable. You know, it's the nature of the system. We do have to convince the majority in order to be able to pass legislation.

HART: The student doesn't have any monopoly on frustration. Get yourself in Congress and you'll have just as high a fever range on that subject as when you were out in the wilderness. All you will get out of the members of Congress is what you would label speeches—until you get a majority of people at home ready to do what the speechmakers suggest we do.

SPENSLEY: Something that bothers me—and I'm directing this at Congressman McCloskey. It's been mentioned that it's necessary for the legislature to bend to the politically feasible solutions. And if we're going to wait until this country decides that the environmental problem is a feasible political thing, isn't that an indictment of the legislature? That it can never be effective in solving the environmental problem?

PAUL McCLOSKEY: When you have mediocrity and unresponsiveness in the legislature, it's because you have mediocrity and apathy in the public that elected that legislature. We elect every congressman every two years. You have it in your power to throw out 435 congressmen next November. But I'll venture to say that most students who are complaining about the problems of this country will do very little in those election campaigns. The McCarthy campaign in New Hampshire, the Harrington campaign in Massachusetts were the first campaigns in which students literally took the effective part that they can. In our own campaign against Shirley Temple, I got 52,000 votes. It turned out that 15,000 of those, almost a third of the votes that I got, were turned out on election day by people your age—high school and college students who went out between four and eight o'clock and caused voters who had not voted yet to vote. Our experience was that each student turned out about ten votes between four and eight o'clock merely by going to people and saying, "Will you come down and vote?" In nearly every case, those people voted for the candidate that that young person asked them to vote for. They were apathetic. They didn't know who the candidates were or what they stood for. The proof of this was, I think, that all day long the county clerk had estimated 60 percent of the voters would turn out. He'd never been wrong. At eight o'clock he found that 69 percent of the voters had voted. He couldn't figure out why. And this amounted to 15,000 extra votes. And we had about 1,500 people your age walking precincts. I think you *can* make this impact. There are two ways this system works. One is in the courts. The other is in the ballot box.

MOGILL: Sure. We can go around and tell people to vote and they'll vote, you know. But we have no means of *choosing* candidates. We have no power to influence the power machinery and, as a result, the issues that we want brought up don't even get brought up. The war in Viet Nam was not an issue in the 1968 election.

HART: I think you've said something more sweepingly than you really intend.

MOGILL: I don't.

HART: It's my impression that you can make an equally strong case that the whole course of the Democratic Party in the 1968 election year was dramatically influenced and affected by youth.

MOGILL: How?

HART: Your test is, you didn't win; my test is, to what degree did you cause positions to be changed, races to be narrowed, and platforms to be pared. And your attitude is that unless your position is accepted in every area, you're a failure.

MOGILL: No.

HART: This was the trend in 1968. In my judgment, history will record that positions were dramatically affected by the attitude and activity of American young people. If I'm wrong on that, I'm wrong on damned near everything I've ever predicted.

MOGILL: And we lost. But what happened was, we were not permitted to bring the issue up, and that's why the whole thing has failed.

OTTINGER: Well, I think that you can take the responsibility for having caused President Johnson not to run for re-election, a man who was considered the most powerful political figure of his day, and then you caused the defeat of Hubert Humphrey in the general election, and you may be sorry you did it now. But that, I think, is the tremendous impact you had. The questions definitely were raised.

MOGILL: Okay. The war *was* an issue in that campaign.

OTTINGER: Oh, the war was a real issue in that campaign. And the reason a lot of people stayed home and the reason a lot of people decided it would be better to have Nixon than Humphrey was because they were disillusioned with Humphrey's actions, attitudes, and pronouncements with respect to the war. It didn't solve the problem of ending the war, but it did change public attitudes enormously. You take a look at the recent Moratorium and the turnout that was had all over this country by citizens never before identified in this. They were turned on by youth. It was one of the most impressive things that has ever happened.

PETERSON: It strikes me that politics expects something different from students than it expects from the public at large. And by this I mean that the number of students who are politically active is probably quite proportionate to the number of adults politically active. The difference I think, to a large extent, is that students are a lot more mobile, and by that I mean they're able to go places where the campaigns are and to have the free time to take a lot of activity upon their shoulders, and to do the work. Now, it seems to me that to say that students have it within their power to change the whole composition of the House of Representatives neglects the fact that it's only a small group of students that would care to try. So I'd like to sort of return this discussion to what we can expect from you people as our representatives. I like to think of you as *our* representatives, because personally, my representatives in Congress I wouldn't claim. I'd like to know what can be done about the seniority system, where you have the heads of very powerful committees, as Senator Hart pointed out, not very interested in the environment, and perhaps supported by vested interests. What can be done about this?

McCloskey: Well, let me try to respond to you. First of all, the seniority system is probably the key element causing unresponsiveness by the Congress to this new priority. And the second element, I would say, is the system of jurisdiction which has been built up over time. In the House, we have at least six committees bearing on the environment, and committee jealousy and jurisdictional fights occupy more of our time—certainly more of the time of the senior members—than does the real work. We are presently in a battle now in the House to determine which committees have jurisdiction over these shining new crusades which the public is so interested in.

But let me mention one encouraging point. The President's reaction and the reaction of Congress in general is to make environment the new priority of the 1970's. And this comes upon them through the public expressions of students and adults and the people back home. In the last four months of the last session, I noticed a tremendous shift in individual congressmen jumping to get aboard the environmental bandwagon. What we need now, in the Congress, is not so much an awareness that the environment rates the high priority and that polluters and manufacturers must take a second priority. What we really need now is the expertise to know which laws passed will affect the environment. And we've found, in many, many cases, that the initial law or the initial concept—the initial answer—has proven wrong. Ecology is not an exact science. The man who developed DDT thought he was helping the environment, I'm sure. So many of the environmental answers may prove under experience to be wrong.

Peterson: I agree that there are questions of expertise that need to be answered. But it does not seem to me that the administration is seriously—since you're a Republican, maybe you could explain this attitude—is seriously interested in answering these questions when the only change it seems to be pursuing is eliminating the name of Edmund Muskie from Department of HEW films, brochures, and so forth. That doesn't seem to me to be a question of expertise.

McCloskey: Well, let me defend the administration briefly in the presence of these very senior Democrats. There were two important passages in the President's State of the Union message—and I haven't heard any commentary by anybody on them. First, he mentioned innovative new ways of financing land acquisition. And if there's one problem in the environment nobody's come up with the answer to, it is the preservation of open space, because every law we've had for 190 years promotes development. So when the President talks about innovative new means of acquiring open space, he's moving into a very, very delicate area which challenges the whole evolution of Anglo-Saxon law. That law says a man's home is his castle and he's entitled to fair compensation if his land is taken. And this is the first indication that this administration may be willing to take the lead and say that when a man's land is taken for public purposes, we pay him for that; but when somebody else's land is benefited by an offramp from a freeway or a rapid transit station, then maybe we'll assess against that man a figure which will aid us to acquire open space. Now, that paragraph in his speech is significant, because that's real leadership—if that's what that paragraph means and if this administration is working on it.

The other idea is a significant one, too. We say we're considering a tax on a product at its source, based on the amount that it will cost ultimately to dispose of it, or on the pollution that it will cause. And when we start proposing a tax of $312 for an automobile at the source because of the air pollution and the waste disposal, that would be a far more realistic means, in my judgment, to end the polluting automobile than any regulatory steps that we might take to ban the internal combustion engine altogether. And that kind of thing in the President's message is indicative of real leadership. And I hope it *will* be leadership, because God knows I think the country is ready to support this kind of leadership. But face it: the people haven't demanded this emphasis on the environment until now. We're expressing the public will when we put leadership in the environment today. Five years ago, this was not true. When I first came to Congress, the Sierra Club was kind of a dirty word among most of the men in the House. It was believed that the lobbying effort that had been put into the Colorado River fight was emotional, was excessive, was extravagant, had been exaggerative of the facts, and because of that, the Sierra Club was not widely respected among most of my colleagues. Today, I think you'd find fewer of them willing to vote against the Sierra Club than, possibly, even the League of Women Voters.

OTTINGER: I'd like to comment on what Pete says. I don't have quite the confidence in the administration's program on the environment that he does. But I think we ought to emphasize that congressmen have an obligation of leadership, too. I think that Pete would agree with that. I mean's he's exercised it. And so have people like Ed Muskie and Gaylord Nelson, Congressman Dingall and Senator Hart.

HART: Let me compliment the administration on its decision to abandon that Everglades jetport. But it wasn't just because the administration was backing abandonment. It was because some of us hooked amendments onto appropriation bills. And we did that because people across the country made clear to us the absolute necessity that this occur. So you can look at that little ruckus and prove that the system is not unresponsive and that everybody, at his particular assignment, does well; or conversely, you can take it and prove that we're all a bunch of fatheads and that it should never have gotten so far.

MOORMAN: The discouraging thing about the jetport case is the fact that there had to be a massive sort of outpouring to stop something for which there had been no massive outpouring whatsoever. You spoke of the land. It strikes me that two things, really, must be done if there's going to be any protection of open space, and one is that there's going to have to be more controls on things which are detrimental to land around the country. And the second thing that has to be done is that Congress has to take the money away from those projects that are facilitating land destruction, such as the Federal Highway Trust Fund. Nothing is going to prevent the destruction of all the open space in the country if the highway program continues at the enormous rate it's going. I think we're just kidding ourselves, otherwise. Do you agree?

MCCLOSKEY: I agree with you. But the great enemy of open space is not the Federal government. It's the local governments. There's no local government in this country that is suited to turn down a new payroll or a new property tax base. Our country's built on a property tax supporting local government. Every impoverished county that has lovely open space, every city that wants to expand is going to permit development. After all, it wasn't the local but the Federal government that got in and stopped the jetport. When you say there was no outpouring for the jetport, what you really mean is there wasn't any sentiment in Florida *against* the jetport.

MOORMAN: It was a Federal program, though—the jetport.

HART: Well, there are other examples of what you're talking about. Certainly government is flat-footed, but so is the fellow who lives on the corner of Lake Erie. Now the threat to Lake Michigan is just as real.

MCCLOSKEY: Let me just say this. We had two days of hearings last December on the question of phosphates in detergents. Here were the two conflicting sides that we got. First of all, about 50 percent, let's say, of all soap powders contain phosphates. Phosphates grow algae; they're one of the best foods algae could possibly have, and they're the primary cause, apparently, of Lake Erie's eutrophication. We have two choices. There are ten million people living in the Lake Erie Basin. One of the suggestions was that we proceed to tertiary treatment sewage plants for all of the Lake Erie Basin. That will cost about $230 million or about $2.30 for each individual living in the basin.

The other suggestion was that we replace the phosphates in soap powder with something called MTA, which is not fully tested, which costs maybe 40 percent more, which would increase the cost of a soap powder by 40 percent to everybody that buys it. Well, it turns out that, according to some figures, each person buys a dollar's worth of phosphates per year. So you're spending $1.40 per head to take the phosphates out at the source, as opposed to sewage treatment at $2.30 a head. This is the kind of specific question before the Congress. Getting tertiary sewage treatment all across the country would run into billions of dollars, so it's obviously impossible in the next decade. We can bitch all we want about the Congress's inaction up until today, but I think, as of now, the Congress is prepared to move and the administration is prepared to move, as fast as the proper choices can be found. But should we spend billions and billions of sewage treatment money to find out that there's an easier and cheaper way to do it?

MOGILL: I'm disturbed about the fact that the Congress has used the environment issue, which is kind of a motherhood-and-apple-pie issue, to ignore the problems of the cities. Not only do all the pollution problems hit the cities and the people who live there in greater magnitude, but the other problems of the cities are just totally being ignored now, and that should not be.

MCCLOSKEY: We operate by a majority vote.

MOGILL: All right. Well, if all the cities burn down, you wouldn't have a majority vote. I'm not telling you what to do because I'm not a congressman and you're a congressman doing what you're doing, but I'm just, you know, pointing out to Congress . . .

MCCLOSKEY: What *are* you doing?

MOGILL: What am I doing? I've been doing a whole lot of things for a number of years, since I've been old enough to do things. Probably a lot of which you would not agree with. I just want to point out to Congress that it seems to be ignoring the problems of the cities these days, and that can't go on, because if it does, you know the consequences as well as I do.

MCCLOSKEY: I quite agree with you. But I suggest, while you're assessing blame to the Congress, that it is the American public that chooses its representation.

And ten-to-one, in the city you speak of that is going down the drain, there is a congressman who gives no attention to the environment. I don't know that to be true, but I would doubt that most people have played any part at all in the electoral process of either selection or the election of the candidates to the Congress, and this is essentially the job and the obligation of the citizen. Isn't it?

MOGILL: Well, then, you're passing the blame one step further.

McCLOSKEY: I'm sharing the blame. I'm trying to say that the blame is as much on the part of the American public as it is on the representatives that they send to Congress.

NAHIKIAN: And it goes much further than just having the technical expertise to clean up air and water. Still, why have we allowed ourselves, as a society, to get into the situation that we're in?

McCLOSKEY: Well, because we put far more priority on the ease and convenience of the automobile than we have ever cared about air pollution. It wasn't till pollution came up and hit a few of us, and hit certain areas of the country so hard, that the American public cared. The primary priority that you and I have had, at least up until two years ago, was how to increase our standard of living and how to increase the number of material goods that we could use—how to make it easier to live, how to have more air conditioning and more power plants to furnish the electricity for air conditioning. Now, we've shifted the priority. But the country at large has shifted that priority and it's fine to sit and apportion the blame, but the real challenge now is what do we do about it. How do we get the hard answers in specific legislative areas?

There have been a few people. Dick Ottinger, here. I came here as a private lawyer five years ago fighting a power line across the countryside. He was one of the few men in the Congress who was willing to get up and battle to cause the Atomic Energy Commission to move that line. This was five years ago. But I can tell you that the great American voter—certainly the great American student, until his sensitivities were alerted by Viet Nam —played no part in the question of priorities. At Stanford University, where I come from, the student body sat on its duff for the last three years and allowed the Stanford Board of Trustees to take the loveliest countryside in the country and turn it into faculty housing.

VOICE: You don't have to worry about student apathy ever again.

HART: I hope you're right, I hope you're right.

SPENSLEY: I asked a question of you for which I really didn't get an answer. I asked if Congress is going to have to wait for the feasible political solution to the problem. And I guess what we're saying is we could never expect Congress to take leadership in trying to solve environmental problems.

HART: Isn't it true that when you talk about Congress taking the leadership, you're asking that a majority identify a method to cure an ill?

SPENSLEY: Well, I . . .

HART: Now, wait a minute. You expect a majority to identify the appropriate response to a social problem and then to vote to adopt and apply the solution. Unless that happens, you say there isn't any leadership. Well, the problems that make up our work record here are so damned complex that short of God and an occasional idiot, everybody admits that nobody knows for sure what to do in most of these areas. It isn't a lack of sensitivity.

SPENSLEY: No, I'm not saying that. I said if Congress has all the informational sources and the expertise to see the problem and to help present the solution to the problem, then we have leadership. Right? But is that what's happening?

McCLOSKEY: Can I try to answer? Let's take a specific instance—the question of population control and explosion. As I recall, it was a number of years ago that the Sierra Club *Bulletin* ran an article saying that any conservationist ought to look at population control as the primary goal because, without it, you couldn't conserve or preserve anything. There was the idea; it was first debated and discussed. Now the Congress has going through it a bill to create a population commission to study the means of limiting population growth. I would expect that the Congress is way ahead of the country as a whole in recognizing the gravity of that problem. If you went into Iowa and Kansas, or anywhere in the areas that elect a majority of our congressmen, population as a problem hasn't even penetrated as yet.

SPENSLEY: Our original premise was that Congress would act in the most politically expedient way. I thought we said that was true, to begin with. It seems like we have a dichotomy.

OTTINGER: Let me try to cope with this if I can, because we face it all the time. You have sitting before you three people who've taken all kinds of risks to do things that are right—that they think are right—regardless of the political feasibility of it. And any one of us may pay the price for it any day. And you've got to make a judgment. To a certain point, you're an effective leader in front of your troops, pulling them along in the direction that you think they ought to go. Then there comes a point—and there are people in Congress who've passed that point, quite clearly—where you're a quixotic, comic figure out there entirely by yourself, leading nobody. Each one of us has to draw that line, and how well we draw it determines whether we're considered exceedingly effective fellows, or whether we're out in the cold. You can expect Congress to lead within those limitations. You can expect a relatively few people to stick their necks out on things that they think are really important. But to achieve major change in this country, under a democratic system, you've got to bring people—I don't say a majority of the people, but a large proportion of them—around. And the alternative is an undemocratic system that I think is very repulsive.

SPENSLEY: Did you ever think of educating the public on an unpopular issue?

MCCLOSKEY: Can I tell you a funny story? I ran for

office opposed to the Viet Nam War, and when I was elected, I thought this meant that the public was opposed to Viet Nam. We took a poll to find out why people voted for me. Five percent of those who voted for me agreed with my Viet Nam position. Eleven percent of those who voted for me disagreed, but voted for me for some other reason. Eighty-four percent of the people who voted for me didn't even know where I stood on the issue. So I don't have a great deal of faith in the sophistication of the voter.

MOORMAN: There was one other question that needs an answer: whether or not there's any way to control the Defense Department's use of defoliants in Viet Nam. They're practicing what appears to be an ecological scorched-earth policy. Is that really necessary? Do we have to convert Laos to a concrete plain just to clear the fields of fire?

OTTINGER: It's possible for public pressure to be brought to change this. But so far, you find very few people who are outraged in this society about the use of this particular technique. They feel that this is something legitimate in warfare. It's not killing people directly, you know, and it's exposing guerrillas and so forth, and so they favor it. There are a group of us in the Congress who've been pointing out the ecological damage that this is doing, and the worldwide consequences that may come about from this. But we are such a minority now. And this is part of the whole question of fundamental democracy that you raised. It isn't right that you or I should be able to do what we think best regardless of what the majority of the people think. It isn't right that we should have that power to go and take this country down an exceedingly unpopular course. But it is our right and our obligation to try to persuade the people that our course is the right one . . .

HART: If I could interrupt. With deep convictions we undertake to make the country turn around, but first we have to have a rather solid conviction that we're right. I mean, in so many of these areas, if you're thoughtful at all, you make a rather tentative suggestion that we turn around. You know, how really confident are we that we know the best way to license television in the public interest?

PETERSON: Yes, but everything points to the fact that we're wrong. At the very minimum we should stop polluting, even if that means stopping industrial growth for a period of a few years. That's simply a minimum level. That doesn't mean cleaning up the mess we've created so far.

HART: Well, let me ask a question in response. The internal combustion engine contributes substantially to air pollution. We should stop building automobiles?

PETERSON: Yes, if that's necessary.

HART: Well, you see, that is a course that we can't persuade, nor would I undertake at the moment to seek to persuade, the Congress to do.

PETERSON: But, you see, we start with all the cards stacked against us. This country's built upon an economic and social structure that's based on pollution. Now, no matter what Congressman McCloskey's belief in students is, I don't think that we have the power to completely overturn the industrial-technocratic society in which we live. And if we do have that power, I think it's going to take so long that the place is going to be devoid of almost any life by the time we succeed.

HART: But unless you educate a majority to that point of view, you never win, do you?

MOGILL: I think it's a real myth that the majority decides anything in this country. Majorities don't decide things. Decisions are made by caucuses of minorities acting, you know, in what they perceive to be the majority's interest.

PETERSON: If a lot of congressmen supported by oil interests or auto interests were more concerned—and I don't mean this to be an indictment of you because I know that your records are very liberal and I really hate to be accusing you three gentlemen, but I can't see how you can defend most of the practices in Congress—so perhaps we do get back to Congressman McCloskey's point that mediocre legislature is the result of a mediocre electorate. But are these people really that short-sighted that they're willing to sell the country down the drain for being reelected in the next election? That's a very discouraging point to reach.

MOORMAN: And a lot of us feel that certain industries are more *equal* than us, you might say . . .

OTTINGER: There is no question about that. There's a power structure in the country today that does bear undue weight in the Congress of the United States, and there's a number of us trying to change that structure.

SIEVERT: What about the time element? I mean, how much time do we have left before we've done so much ineradicable damage that it can't be undone? Is there time to educate people? Do we have any time?

OTTINGER: Well, we're faced with very ugly alternatives. One alternative is throwing out democracy. So the answer is we've got to put every ounce of energy that we have into educating the country fast, and we're going to be aided by our own slowness, because we're going to have some catastrophes. We had a catastrophe in California with the oil. We're going to have some air pollution catastrophes in our major cities very shortly and people are going to start getting killed by the droves. And we just hope that these relatively restricted catastrophes are going to be enough to wake up this country in time so we don't have any widespread ecological disasters.

HART: Let me return to Dr. MacMullan. Dr. Mac-Mullan said we have ten years to save mankind. By that, he means that the 70's will be a decade of decision. We will take or fail to take the action which will determine whether people will inhabit the earth very far beyond the decade. He lists the dangers: famine, resource depletion, pollution, nuclear war. And he suggests that not one of them alone will destroy us, but that a combination will, unless, within the decade, we act. Of course, we could be more optimistic if we could identify the benign and all-wise dictators to whom we could turn over the decade. But I prefer to think, instead, that we will act.

PART IX

the learning process

"It is not the fault of young people that science is now widely viewed with hostility, as an insensitive instrument devoid of humanistic values. This is a picture that scientists themselves, perhaps inadvertently, helped to create."

by Everett M. Hafner

Toward a New Discipline for the Seventies: Ecography

Seven-tenths of the way through the twentieth century, we have suddenly discovered that man may be breeding and poisoning himself out of existence. Man's problems of food shortages, limited mineral resources, water and air pollution, energy consumption, chemical and radioactive contamination, noise generation and deforestation now seem to be growing faster than the growing population itself. Suddenly we have become aware that our attack on the environment is an attack upon ourselves. Even as our technology expands, it threatens the physical and mental health of men everywhere. Now we are beginning to see that a dramatic change in man's attitude toward himself and his planet is necessary if he is to survive.

Each of us has his own dreadful vision, his scenario as it were, of what could happen to us if we continue along our present course. A brief but violent nuclear war, brought on by the rage and frustration of hungry millions or by tyranny or even by simple ineptitude—

Everett M. Hafner is dean of the School of Natural Sciences and Mathematics of Hampshire College, Amherst, Massachusetts. Portions of this chapter are excerpted from Professor Hafner's address at the American Association for the Advancement of Science symposium on undergraduate studies in environmental science, December, 1969.

this is the most familiar fantasy. Mine is very different, and in some respects more dreadful. It is based loosely on our recent observations of Venus, a planet of Earth-like size, but whose atmosphere is grotesquely different from ours. In my image, the cloud of dense water and carbon dioxide enveloping that planet is the result of massive pollution of the air from runaway processes started by an ancient technology.

In the light of what we now know about ourselves and the natural world, the story of what might have happened on Venus a billion years ago is not unbelievable. It might have gone like this:

Life evolved from lower to higher forms in a warm but otherwise benign habitat; an intelligent species arose to exploit its resources for the sake of power and growth; a point was reached where the balance of life was endangered by insults to the environment. Increasing amounts of carbon dioxide in the atmosphere, coming from large-scale combustion of hydrocarbons, began to raise the temperature of the planet through the familiar "greenhouse" effect until it became clear to all thinking creatures that life itself would soon be threatened. Despite the most imaginative efforts on the part of her scientists to alleviate the problem, Venus grew steadily less habitable as the temperature rose. A strange and uncontrollable panic gripped the planet, leading eventually to the revival of old and discredited superstitions. One of these had been the worship of Earth, a blue and beautiful neighbor in the sky, long recognized by scientists as an abode of life and a possible haven for the overpopulated societies of Venus.

By the time the crisis came, it was already too late to develop more than the most pathetic and abortive efforts to send significant colonies of Venutians to Earth. Instead, under the spell of the new religion, engineers designed a monstrous project to alter the spin of their planet. Their idea was to placate the God of Earth by keeping him always in view of their major continent. To accomplish this, huge jets were erected on the equator and enormous amounts of fuel were burned for many years to slow down, and ultimately to reverse, the rotation of Venus. When the engines finally burned out, more than one percent of the total mass of the planet had been converted into carbon dioxide and water, constituting the atmosphere as we now see it. And Venus was dead.

I do not mean to propose this as a serious theory for the explanation of the atmosphere of Venus or of its strange and anomalous rotation. I am only suggesting something that is within the realm of possibility not only for the history of that planet, but also for our own future. We are already well along the road toward irreversible change in the quality of the Earth, brought about by our own insatiable greed and our inability to control our habit of breeding for maximum size. If we reach a point of no return, it is not inconceivable to me that we shall react to the pressure of a variety of frightening circumstances by going mad as a species. Then Earth, too, may grow a dense opaque atmospheric shroud which, for all I know, is the sign of the death of planets.

Fortunately, we seem to have some time left to reverse the march toward the destruction of our world. We are also fortunate in witnessing the emergence of a new generation of young people deeply concerned for a wide range of social problems and equipped with energy and good sense to act out their roles as responsible citizens. I have had the privilege of meeting and working with many students who represent the movement toward a restoration of the environment, and I am convinced that they deserve all of the help that we can find for them. My own small contribution to them is a proposal that they learn to think of science in a broader and more comfortable sense than their academic and social experience has so far accustomed them to. It is, of course, not the fault of young people that science is now widely viewed with hostility, as a cold and insensitive instrument whose work is devoid of or even antagonistic to social and humanistic value. This is a picture that scientists themselves, perhaps inadvertently, have helped to create. But we are beginning to see vigorous signs of a change.

While much of the traditional hard science of the past is now losing support, the areas of science which bear most heavily on the condition of man are now coming strongly forward. First among them is ecology, the branch of biology which deals with mutual relations between organisms and their environment. It is a science with a long and venerable history, but only recently, in the presence of acute distress in the ecology of man, has it come to prominence with the sense of excitement and promise that I recall when nuclear physics burst upon us more than three decades ago. But ecology by itself, even with strong emphasis on the human species, will not be sufficient to handle the grave problems that confront us now, since many of these problems have their roots in social and political behavior. What we need is a new field of science standing midway between what we now recognize as the natural sciences and the social sciences, combining insights of both yet developing its own fundamental technique. Science without a sense of social commitment will always be a part of academic life, but it will not answer the gravest questions now before us. And political action, however wisely and humanely directed, will fail equally if it is uninformed by science.

History tells us that ideas, like organisms, follow a pattern of evolution that we would do well to understand. In religion, in philosophy, in art and music and literature, and in history itself, newborn ideas may or may not be strong enough to mature, and wise enough to age gracefully. Mutation and replication are working processes in the history of ideas, as are symbiosis, parasitism, slow disease and sudden death.

Communities of ideas, gathered together around central themes deeply rooted in human consciousness, form the "disciplines" of academic life. At a given stage of our development, each academic discipline represents a consensus on questions of priority, feasibility, research technique, continuity, and academic prestige. The disciplines, like their constituent ideas, have natural cycles of life. And the enterprise of learning works best when we nurse and nourish the newborn, while burying the dead with minimum expense and ceremony.

Nowhere are these processes more vivid than in the history of science. My own most familiar discipline, physics, regarded sometimes as a central kingdom in the larger world of natural science, formed itself slowly and painfully from a set of powerful ideas in philosophy, mathematics, astronomy, experimental design, chemistry, engineering and military science. Galileo sensed the birth of discipline when he constructed dialogues on "Two New Sciences," but it was not until much later that physics emerged in recognizable form. Even now there is some difficulty with its definition: there are dictionaries that describe it in negative terms only, as "the study of inanimate matter in which no chemical change occurs." There is also extraordinary variety in the work that physicists do, from bottom to top of the energy scale and from the smallest to the largest of natural systems. Yet it is fair to say that physicists share more than a label and a professional society; they collect around a set of problems and modes of inquiry most usefully identified as a single discipline. This may, by the way, not always continue to be so.

If physics were forming today, we should of necessity have to see it as "interdisciplinary," since physicists would not yet exist. Academic departments of philosophy, mathematics, and so on, would be uncomfortable hiding places for people concentrating on the study of energy for its own sake. A university here and there, supported by grants from special panels of the National Science Foundation, would set up a Center for Research on the Laws of Motion (CRLM), devoted mainly to graduate studies directed by the faculties of various schools and departments. Undergraduate students, sensing a crisis of leadership, would devote summer and weekend to mechanics and radioactivity. The AAAS would sponsor symposia on ways of organizing these activities into respectable courses and programs.

It is in this perspective that I see our present concern for the development of environmental science. My own mail—hundreds of papers and reports, dozens of books, thousands of letters—brings me mounting news of responsible and intelligent concern for the future of the earth as a home for life, and of proposals for tooling up in response to that concern. Indeed, the flood of paper through my office is a small environmental crisis in itself. Although some of what I read is simple-minded or self-serving or otherwise useless, the mainstream is strong and full of honest purpose.

Something else is happening. An enormous academic movement, supported by students of all kinds from the most to the least revolutionary, by faculty in all areas of study, by deans and presidents and authoritative figures in government, is pulling us forward. The movement is so strong as to be hazardous in itself. Garrett Hardin tells us of the dangers of a "euphoria . . . likely to make us lower our critical guard, to indulge in ill-considered or irresponsible leadership." Much depends, especially for the long future of environmental action, on the development of informed leaders.

This brings me to my point. It seems inescapable that environmental science is interdisciplinary. And so it is, in the sense that it connects almost all fields of study, ranging from architecture to zoology. But chemistry or mathematics or economics is interdisciplinary in the same sense; in my brief history of physics, I do not suggest that its emergence as a discipline removes it from contact with everything else. On the contrary, and paradoxically, intensive concentration on the fundamental laws of nature clarifies our view of the whole world of reason, in a way that would be impossible otherwise. The lesson of experience, perhaps explicable in psychological terms, is that specialization is essential to our progress. A sense of discipline, a devotion to a concentrated community of closely related ideas, is our most productive scholarly tool.

Given this principle, we might well consider a new

discipline within environmental science. I wish to call it "Ecography" as a way of recognizing that it is new, and as a suggestion of its basic meaning. The name is unimportant, but the conception of discipline is vital.

Instead of listing the dozens of existing disciplines from which ecography has grown, let us simply ask about its central and deeply rooted theme. We are engaged in a study of facts and values which describe and control man's interaction with his habitat. In what respect, then, does ecography differ from human ecology or, for that matter, geography as it is currently understood? The answer is that ecology, for its own scholarly purposes, must carry too great a burden of biology, while geography must carry too little. If you wish, ecology is too close to the exclusively natural sciences while geography is too close to the social sciences. Thus the role of ecography, as its name suggests, is to establish a disciplinary beachhead in what appears to be a critical no-man's land between the two cultures of science.

I earnestly believe that the new discipline has already been born, but that it is a foundling, crying for adoption. In view of the rapidly growing severity of man's ecological crisis, we—students and teachers alike—cannot afford to overlook the chance that our new baby is a *wunderkind* whose future strength depends upon our feeding him properly now.

The colleges and universities must take action. In the case of the multiversities, whose structures are rigid and jealously guarded, it is neither feasible nor necessary to build interdisciplinary centers in order to provide an ecographical setting. The better way is for each to organize its Department of Ecography with the usual spectrum of people and facilities: the chairman, the faculty, the budget, the laboratory, the undergraduate and graduate programs, and the degrees. It is only through the conventional structure, which has worked so well for other disciplines of science, that most universities can respond to the demand for professional recognition now building up among young students and teachers. And this is certainly one way in which our environmental problems can be adequately studied and —hopefully—ultimately solved.

Perhaps there is a better way, open only to institutions newly forming and therefore free from prior structural commitment. They can listen to Robert Hutchins, criticizing our universities:

> Civilization and culture cannot be preserved and expanded without another institution that is missing. Today we have no centers of independent thought and criticism. The multiversity is not independent: it is the result of the parallelogram of forces at work in the community. It is not engaged as an institution in thought or criticism . . . It is compartmentalized both vertically and horizontally into departments and divisions that are in competition for money and students. A multipurpose institution can by definition have no unifying principle.

Instead, says Hutchins, we must look to the college, or cluster of colleges, in which departments of study are never permitted to organize. The college is a small community of teachers and students, using their special talents to achieve clearly defined goals. It is possible, even necessary, in such a setting to combine a sense of discipline with the respectability of change. A new discipline, like ecography, can find a natural and immediate place; so can an old one, like chemistry. And some disciplines can be permitted to die without endangering the lives (or livelihoods) of people.

Whatever modes of reform they choose to adopt, the colleges and universities of the world will be moving toward this new discipline in response to a variety of forces. One is the emergence of ecography as an interesting and challenging subject of study. Another is the collective voice of thousands of students, demanding academic recognition of their concern. But the greatest force is the threat of our own destruction, which we must continue to face until the gap between the sciences is filled.

by David Jeffrey and Glenn Kageyama

Innovating Relevant Curricula

In the winter quarter of 1969, a new course entitled
"Population: The Vital Revolution" was offered at the
University of California at Irvine. It was unique for
several reasons. Undergraduates organized and administered it. It was incorporated into the curricula of both
the Schools of Biological and Social Sciences. And it
dealt with the most urgent problem facing mankind
today, from a totally interdisciplinary approach.

The basic idea for the course had come from a few
highly interested students possessing some knowledge of
the population problem. The number of enthusiastic
students soon grew; from their combined efforts a tentative proposal was drawn up on paper to present to the
dean. Although we had discussed the course idea
already with him, it was important that our proposal
was as well-organized, thorough, and specific as we
could possibly make it. The proposal contained the
purpose of the course and its social implications; the
method of presentation as a lecture series; a tentative
course outline indicating the general subject matter to
be covered; credit value of the course and in what
departments (biology and social science); tentative
course requirements such as assignments and tests; the
approximate size of enrollment desired; the method of

David Jeffrey and Glenn Kageyama are graduate students at the
University of California.

evaluating students; a tentative bibliography of suggested readings, and a brief statement of financial feasibility. We had learned from informal personal contact that the course idea was enthusiastically received by students, faculty, and administration. So we included written statements of support from members of those groups along with the proposal to the dean, plus a statement summarizing the results of our informal survey.

Our proposal was accepted.

To avoid administrative complications, a faculty member in the School of Biological Sciences registered the course under his name. It was responsibility in name only, because the organizing students had charge of the course. In our second phase of planning, the group worked through the university registrar to establish the size of classroom, credit value of the course, class meeting times, the prerequisites (none, we decided), a course description for the quarterly course listing, and official registration in the university curricula by title and number.

A more detailed course outline (with topics suggested for each lecture) was drafted, not with the intention of "structuring" all the lectures but to give some continuity to the material covered and minimize the possibility of repetition.

Next, we tentatively selected qualified specialists to lecture. Most of these individuals were from the Irvine campus; in selecting ones from other schools and the professions, we had to consider the expenses involved. Then, with voluntary student secretarial help, we sent a letter to each prospective lecturer, inviting him to participate, and covering these points: a course introduction and statement of purpose, the tentative course outline, time/date/location of the lecture, a statement (if necessary) saying that travel expenses and honoraria would be arranged pending an affirmative response. We made certain to include a request for other qualified specialists in case the invitee couldn't accept, and a self-addressed, stamped postcard.

After acceptances had come in, we mailed the lecturers any changes, additional information, requests for a suggested bibliography and for permission to tape record their lectures. Then we arranged transportation and room and board for off-campus lecturers, and the use of any necessary instructional media such as tape recorders and projectors.

The overall cost of the course, including transportation, room, board, and honoraria for off-campus specialists, and miscellaneous administrative expenses, came to approximately $600. The money came from the School of Biological Sciences (a certain amount of funds is allotted to every course in the curriculum), individual departments (whenever an outside lecturer also presented a seminar for their departments), and student body funds (after submission of a fairly detailed request for financial aid to the Associated Student Body Government).

For publicity, we sent letters explaining "Population: The Vital Revolution" and its goals to deans of all university schools, the vice chancellor of academic affairs, the chancellor, the director of public relations, university and community newspapers, the student body president, the president of the academic senate, and several community groups, like the Business Associates of the University of California Kiwanis Club, that were interested in university activities.

Two of the student organizers administered the course. Their responsibilities included making the introductory statements at the beginning of the course, introducing each lecturer, being "host" to off-campus lecturers, representing the course in public relations matters, writing thank-you letters to the lecturers, and administering assignments, suggested readings, and the final examination. Since considerable time and effort was involved, the two students were given full course credit for their work by the dean.

All courses in the university curricula are required to have a final examination so that its students may be evaluated in some way for transcript records. However, our final examination evolved into more of a question-naire than an exam. Due to the enormous quantity of material presented from a wide spectrum of disciplines, we felt that an examination requiring a regurgitation of facts would be arcane. Instead, students were asked very general questions related to their understanding of the overall problems of overpopulation. And because the purpose of the course was to stimulate environmental awareness, they were asked for a personal evaluation of the measure of that success. They were also asked to suggest course changes or improvements for the next quarter, and to write letters expressing their environmental ideas to persons or institutions with influence and power. Consequently, letters were mailed to newspapers, magazines, television and radio stations, the President of the U.S., Congressmen, Senators, the United Nations, even the Pope.

To perpetuate the course, we established a form of apprenticeship. The apprentice organizers we had recruited aided in the course organization for the first quarter, and were then given the responsibility for it during the following quarter. The original organizers served only as counselors.

The course content—the quality of information presented—in the final analysis determines any course's success. An outline of ours is presented here as a possible guideline for those planning a similar course.

Population: The Vital Revolution

Lecture I.   *The Growth of World Population*

Time and evolution of life on earth; emergence of man; history of human population growth; explanation of human population growth curve; the world situation today, by continents; a look at the future.

II. *The History of Man and Energy*

The concept of energy (energy systems, efficiency); man the hunter (origin of society, fire, origin of speech, tools and weapons, clothing, food storage and shelter); agricultural revolution (domestication of plants and animals, origin of cities); communication revolution (innovation of movable type); scientific and industrial revolution (use of inanimate energy, innovation of mass production, automation); energy sources (present demands, outlook for the future).

III. *The Geography of Man and His Resources*

Physical world of man (properties and classification of soils, geographic distribution of soil types, climatic regions of the world, geographic distribution of water and mineral resources, geographic distribution of vegetation); geography of man (environment and culture).

IV. *The Principles of Ecology*

Ecology; populations; communities; ecosystems; concept of the niche; energy flow (food chains, biotic pyramids); chemical cycles; environmental feedback.

V. *Water*

Properties of water; distribution of water; hydrologic cycle; industrial and urban uses of water; nonconsumptive water uses (waterpower for electricity, water for recreation); water for the future.

VI. *Photosynthesis*

Importance of photosynthesis (source of food and energy for all living organisms, source of oxygen); process of photosynthesis; photosynthetic limitations of the earth.

VII.   Food and Nutrition

Essential food elements and their sources (salt, vitamins, amino acids, etc.); malnutritional diseases; effects of malnutrition on ability to think, work and resist disease; geography of caloric production and consumption; geography of hunger and malnutrition; possibilities of increasing world food production; the coming famines (India today).

VIII.   History of Disease and Medicine

Geographic history of epidemics (the Black Death, other historical epidemics); development of public health and medicine; effect of public health and medicine on death control; medicine for tomorow; artificial transplants; regulation of aging.

IX.   Pollution and Overexploitation

Pollution of air, land and water resources (chemical and gaseous wastes, radioactive wastes, pesticides and poisons, thermal pollution); how pollutants are formed and circulated (concentration phenomenon of toxic substances by living organisms); overexploitation of natural resources (fishery and wildlife resources; land and water resources; forest resources; fossil fuel resources).

X.   Population Dynamics

The composition of a human population and differential fertility (sex and age pyramids, race, nationality and language; rural/urban characteristics; religious affiliation; educational, economic and marital status); natality; mortality; migration; aging process in a population; demographic transition; DC (developed country) and UDC demographic behavior; theories on population growth (natural theories: Malthus, Sadler, Doubleday, Spencer, Gini; social theories: Godwin, Marx, George, Dumont, Garr-Saunders); population trends of the world.

XI. Socio- and Psychobiology

Natural mechanisms of population control in living organisms (competition for water in plants; predation, food shortage and disease as animal controls; territoriality and social behavior as animal controls); population density and social pathology (stress in animals, stress in man); basic human needs and the effects of overpopulation (food, security, land, etc.); mind and mood control; impact of discoveries in psychobiology.

XII. Birth Control

Reproductive cycle (hormones, etc.); early practices of population control (restrictive practices: infanticide, abortion, sexual taboos, treatment of aged and ill, acceptance of disaster, war marriage restrictions, migration and contraception; expansive practices: larger resources, need for defense, dynastic and national interest and religion; eugenic practices); present practices of population control (family planning; abortion; contraceptive techniques: IUD, rhythm, disc, condom, sterilization, immunization; the Pill and its impact).

XIII. Man and the Control of Evolution

Fundamentals of genetics; human genetics and genetic diseases; genetic control (of food crops, domesticated animals and human populations); genetic warfare.

XIV. Cities and Urbanization

Origin and development of society; birth and evolution of cities; emergence of the metropolis; urbanization of the world; urban problems (housing, recreation and education, class conflict, other socio-economic problems); megalopolis—future city of man.

XV. Economic Problems

Population and production vs. consumption; law of diminishing returns; human needs and the scarcity of resources; problems of unemployment; problems of education; problems of economic development in underdeveloped countries; present trends in economic development and living standards in various countries.

XVI. *Political Problems*

International problems of overpopulation (threat to peace, threat to democracy, political instability); domestic problems of internal conflict; present destructive capacity of bacterial and chemical agents.

XVII. *Technological Potential in a Growing World*

Extraterrestrial resources; marine resources; living under the sea; impact and potential use of the computer; new advances in transportation and communication; possibilities of meeting tomorrow's energy demands.

XVIII. *Biology and Public Policy*

Biological revolution and its impact on society; public policy.

XIX. *Human Nature and the Fate of Mankind*

Evolution of human thought (ideas that have changed man's thinking); cultural and religious attitudes on birth control; psychological barriers; human nature (what man needs and what he wants); evolution and the fate of mankind.

XX. *Policies of the Past, Present, and Future*

Past and present policies of the U.S. (Public Law 480 and other policies); policies of other countries and their attitudes toward the U.S.; suggested policies for the future; the need to educate.

Postview and Course Evaluation

"Population: The Vital Revolution" was a stunning success in its very first quarter. In his post-evaluation, one student commented: "This course gave me hope for education. It forced me to think and act." Another felt that the course could be best taught only as it had been, with a series of lectures by prominent speakers who were experts in their respective fields. Further, the fact that all speakers did not agree completely on every aspect was appreciated by the students, for it gave each class member the opportunity to weigh facts and reach his own conclusions.

Practically the only criticism of the course was that it reached too small an audience; that it ought to have been offered in some form to the community at large.

by Norah Wylie

The Environmental Forum

In keeping with its new role as a social force, the university today is becoming increasingly committed to the fight to save the environment. The presence of top scientists and researchers on many campuses, coupled with the current trend of student activism, makes the university an excellent starting point for a variety of environmental programs and campaigns. An example of one of these programs is a course called the Environmental Forum, offered at the State University of New York at Albany. Designed to inform students, faculty members, and citizens of the surrounding community of the ecological crisis, the course draws on experts from various science and social science departments to appear as lecturers. Along with these guest lecturers, panelists from related fields and industries appear to offer positive or negative criticisms of the major speech, and to answer the audience's questions.

The Forum was originally conceived as an expression of the ecological conscience of the university, and to generate environmental concern not only on campus but in the cities of Albany, Schenectady, and Troy and in the surrounding rural centers. Education alone is not the major emphasis of the course; the need for immediate action and reform is heavily stressed. The course requires each student to submit a proposal for an "action

Norah Wylie is an English major at the State University of New York at Albany.

project" which is to be completed as soon as possible, a project which either researches a specific problem and proposes a solution, or a project designed to "spread the word" and involve more people in campaigns to rehabilitate and protect the environment. These projects are important because of the ends they can accomplish; they are also interesting because of the attitudes and philosophies revealed in the approaches taken by the students involved in the projects.

One of the most conspicuous trends is the reliance on visual aids to "spread the word." Many of the projects rely on animated cartoons, film clips, or photographic essays to make an impact on the public. It is as if the immediacy of the problems makes them manageable only through the use of the most contemporary medium and art form, the film. With little or no writing included in these projects, they attempt to arrest the viewer in the middle of everyday life, shocking him out of his blissfully unaware state by appealing to him visually. Tom Murphy, for example, illustrates the dangers of jet exhausts in an uncomplicated 30-second film clip accompanied by a minimum of dialogue. The film shows a plane discharging heavy black smoke and obliterating the sun. The warning: "In 1984 you will be able to get from New York to London in 45 minutes—but it will be just as dark over there." Becky Masland, in a series of animated cartoons, lends a somewhat more humorous touch to an examination of the negative effects of technology, but manages to get the point across in the same efficient manner Murphy uses in his film. Barbara Gerzonick has produced a photographic essay of industrial pollution on various waterways in New York State, and is preparing this essay for a televised presentation.

Along with the visual-aid method of educating the public, several students have developed oral presentations for audiences, giving short descriptions of a pollution situation. A large number of these presentations are geared for junior high and high school levels rather than a college or adult audience. The hope is to reach students and get them working at a relatively young age.

This attention to the high school audience reveals the belief of the Forum students that all age and interest groups must work together for the clean-up of the environment, for no single group alone can effect the necessary changes.

Presentations for the high school audiences vary from short speeches suggesting possible courses of action to an interdepartmental course intended to foster an awareness of ecological problems. Dan Perlmutter, a senior geography major at Albany, has given a short talk at Linton High School in Schenectady suggesting possibilities for action by the students themselves, and the necessity of gaining the support of their parents in any of their programs. At another area high school, Joseph Slack has started an "environmental club" with a drive to collect aluminum cans as its initial project. The action project will help students understand some of the problems of solid waste disposal.

Marion Collins, a teacher at Albany High School, has developed a year-long course called Environmental Studies for her junior classes. The course stresses the necessity of understanding modern pollution problems from beginning to end, rather than concentrating on the present-day situation alone. Creating an awareness of the values of urban environment occupies a large part of Mrs. Collins's program. She uses such devices as walking-tours through urban neighborhoods and analyses of city development programs to acquaint her students with situations that exist in their own back yards. The goal of these studies is to give the student an understanding of how to start solving problems before they reach a crisis point.

Other Forum participants are carrying the message to the general public. Doug Williams, Steve Rothe and Joe Slack, for example, are working through radio stations in the Albany area. Doug has already used eight hours of prime radio time to define pollution problems, and has arranged for twenty hours more.

Betty Spurgeon, an architecture student at Rensselaer Polytechnic Institute, makes use of another channel of

public information. She has written two articles which
have appeared in local newspapers. The articles deal
with urban renewal and the destruction of historic buildings. Articles of this type serve the essential function of
reminding people that there is a man-made as well as a
natural environment to be considered and protected.
Beth Goldmacher has written four one-act plays dealing
with overpopulation. They were to have been produced
by another student, Marty Feldman, in conjunction with
the Environment Teach-In. Neil Linden is in the process
of completing two songs, based on traditional folk mel-
odies, with lyrics commenting on the contemporary
crisis. In the field of plastic arts, Guido Bida has constructed a water fountain-sculpture to illustrate the need
for purifying existing water supplies.

Underlying most of these projects is the conviction
that the means of our consumption must be changed.
Glen Dionne and Gary Slutsky, two R.P.I. architecture
students, recognize that the problem is not technology
but man's use and misuse of it. They have therefore proposed to study alternate methods of producing energy
and running technological systems. One alternative: an
updating of once-used techniques, such as windmills and
waterwheels.

The Environmental Forum has been successful in a
way few courses are ever visibly successful: it has
changed the lives of the participants on a practical level.
By completing their projects, by establishing a Protect
Your Environment (PYE) Club on campus, by participating in the Governor's Youth Conference in New
York City, the members of the Forum have taken action
against the wanton destruction of the environment. The
long-range effects of the Forum—and of programs like
it—will be visible over the period of the next few decades, and these effects will be measured by nothing less
than the quality of our total environment.

PART X

endpieces

"And in the windows of World War II hung the banners of the blue star families, with boys-at-arms overseas. Now we could have green star families if the old man gets his vasectomy and rides a bike to work instead of that 4,000 pound Super-Polluter Eight."

by Alan Gussow

Where Life-Style Counts, Who Needs Nature?

I have been somewhat rudely awakened to the possibility that those of us concerned with the environment are in some cases asking the wrong questions. We begin by observing that the world is changing and we proceed from there to ask, if we are morally inclined, what we can do to "correct" or direct change. If we are thrifty, we inquire what can be done to prevent waste. If we are planners, we ask what can be done to "improve" cities. If we are nature lovers, we ask how can nature be introduced into urban lives and locations; and if we are admirers of open spaces, we ask how people can be made to support population control and easements in equal doses.

Whatever their phrasing, the questions we are asking are based on the assumption that we already know in a broad general sense what should be done to make cities more liveable, and even the biological and psychological reasons why it should be done, so that the only questions which remain to be answered have to do with how this transformation is to be achieved. I would like to propose here that our view of what needs doing, while it may be ultimately correct, may not be as universally

Alan Gussow is both artist *and* writer. A Hudson River conservationist, he pioneered the National Park Service's artist-in-residence program.

agreed upon, nor in the short run as desirable, as we have tended to assume.

Some time ago, I was invited to serve as a visiting lecturer at the University of Massachusetts School of Landscape Architecture. Ten black architecture students from the Hampton Institute in Virginia were guests of the university in a two-week exchange program which saw the black students paired off with the white University of Massachusetts landscape architects to develop a plan for metropolitan Springfield. I gave a long and rambling talk which generally focused on the importance of place, and on how I felt we were products of our places. I suppose I was guilty, as we all are to some extent, of generalizing out of my own experience. I talked of what it had meant to me to grow up on Long Island when you could still roam the undeveloped fields and walk winters on the deserted sand bars of Jones Beach. I spoke of the sharp delineations of seasons in Vermont where I went to college—of April mudtime, of the endless, agonizing wait for spring. And I reminisced about light in European places—about the apricot sunsets in Rome, the sharp-edged lucidity of Athenian noons and the way the sun caressed and softened the stern temple carvings in Egypt.

If there was a thread running through my remarks, it was that people are physical, that we all live somewhere, and that the "whereness" affects us, forms our outlook, gives shape to our values. When I finished, confident that I had been heard and that the group had at least remained awake and responsive, I asked a leading question. What of all that I said did they most disagree with? Where had I really gone wrong? A black student wasted no time. "All this talk about place," he said, "about the importance of place. Man, that's not what I care about. Hell no, it's not place that counts. It's life-style."

The next three hours were an education for all of us. There were lots of thing they didn't like, though they didn't always agree on what they were. Some of the Hampton men simply opted for change, any change, as an improvement. "As long as it's different from what they've got now, as long as it's a change, it's going to be okay," was one black student's comment. They objected to planners who were tourists, planners who passed through, observed, took photographs, made maps, made plans, but who never really shared the lives they were planning for. Some said that what was wrong with city plans was that they created middle class patterns for the lower classes to live with (though they were uncertain as to the values that could characterize a genuinely responsive "lower class" project, in contrast to the middle class values of orderliness and neatness that characterized many present renewal programs).

There was at least one point on which the blacks agreed. They agreed that they were indifferent to the amenities the white students and I considered critical for the liveability, even the survival of the city. Their environmental view was not ecological. It was social. Open malls and parks, greenbelts and recreation areas—they found these secondary, almost trivial. They had a priority list on which life-style ranked higher than place. Place was important only because it was where life happened. Aesthetics and nature were secondary.

The afternoon was a behaviorist's dream. At the same time, it was an ecologist's nightmare. Where did it leave me and my conviction that there was a future for nature in the city of man? I had come to Amherst a lover of open space and was now confronted by black architects telling me open space had no significant relationship to life-style.

Here was a confrontation which threatened my most basic assumptions—that nature was necessary, that open space was essential, that the struggle to improve the air and reduce noise was critical to our well-being. And here was a group of bright, young black urban architectural students saying they couldn't care less. What I saw as the city's intrinsic problems, they were saying were certainly not even major concerns to those who inhabited the city's least satisfying and least aesthetic areas. And it was made very clear that to ignore the values and attitudes of the urban blacks was to run the risk that my solutions, and the solutions of those who felt as I did, would be ignored. This is not to suggest that others hadn't earlier come to the same conclusions as I did. What I am suggesting, however, is that those of us who believe in the importance of nature must ask, and answer, a tough question: is natural open space as we perceive it truly important in the daily lives of city residents?

When we consider the "importance" of open space, we can obviously cite first the contribution that it makes to our biological well-being by renewing the air, cleaning the water and providing light for the growing of plants. But isn't its greater value more sociological than biological? With all respect to Lewis Mumford's idea of the Garden City, it appears unlikely, at best, that we could build enough greenery into our cities to provide adequately for biological needs which must in the end be met by world-wide environmental planning. I am not concluding that urban residents have any less need for clean air and pure water. I am only emphasizing that cities must be placed in proper ecological context as a part—and only a part—of a broader picture.

Given cities as they are—an overwhelming concentration of sounds, signs and smells of human life—open space can play a unique role within the city. Open space can relieve the stress. Even the black architectural students who were indifferent to nature in the city understood the role of urban open space as *cooling-off* space. Indifference to nature as a value did not mean they were unaware of the function of open space in social terms. Indeed, the stress created in cities was not always viewed as something negative, something to be overcome. A few of the black architects—notably those who grew up in cities—described their ideal "new town" in very urban terms. What they wanted to see in planned communities, for example, was human diversity—the sight of people, lots of people, interacting not only with the place but with each other. What was sought was the indefinable pulse of city life, a cadence produced only where people congregated. One student from South Philadelphia summed up his perfect place, saying, "What I want is all the action of the slum without ugliness. It's a question of degree. Go far enough—enough people, the right momentum and a city is just fine. A little too much and you got hell. If I had my way I'd make new towns feel like a city that knew when to stop. Suburbs? That's like living in a graveyard!" By this definition, open space can help cities "know when to stop" by limiting human density. None of the foregoing, however, places any particular value on nature, as opposed to open space.

The more difficult question is whether there is a need for "nature" in the city. We know that the human organism seems to be infinitely adaptable. Yet how much noise is too much? How much crowding is too much? We also know that cities create their own microclimates —hotter and rainier than the surrounding regions. Yet people survive, or at least seem to. The issue isn't survival really; it is one of adaptability. And in the end it isn't so much a question of physical adaptability. It is primarily a question of spiritual and emotional adaptability. Natural open space—call it nature in the city— can sustain not just the human species, but more importantly, the humanness in the species. And if nature makes us more human, it more than justifies its presence in the city of man. Ian McHarg understood this clearly when he wrote:

Perhaps in the future, analysis of those factors which contribute to stress disease will induce inquiry into the values of privacy, shade, silence, the positive stimulus of natural materials and the presence of comprehensible order, indeed natural beauty. When young babies lack fondling and mother love, they sometimes succumb to moronity and death. The dramatic reversal of this pattern has followed simple maternal solicitude. Is the absence of nature—its trees, water, rocks and herbs, sun, moon, stars and changing seasons—a similar type of deprivation? The solicitude of nature, its essence if not its image, may be seen to be vital.

The "mothering" by nature that McHarg refers to should not be from an absentee mother. It is no comfort to the slum dweller to know that the Grand Canyon cleaves Arizona. It is the immediate neighborhood place that exerts the strongest influence on how one feels and on what one becomes.

We *are* products of our places. In the way food nourishes our body, our environment feeds our dreams. The houses we have lived in, the schools we have attended—and if we are fortunate, the summer vacations, the warmth, light, mist, moods; and if we are less fortunate, the crowding, the stench, the rats—all the places we have experienced combine in our minds and contribute to that unique organism which is each of us. And in the end, it is not the exotic or foreign or the occasional place that most affects us. It is the familiar, the random observations in our ordinary life that most shape our point of view.

So the fact remains that the major contribution of open space in the city is not to oxygenate the air but to relieve the experiential stultification of the "fixed" environment and to reduce the pressures of the human environment. I say this in spite of the fact that the black architectural students argued first for social interaction. In animal studies, the more variable the animal's environment, the more alert, flexible and able it is to cope with change. By denying our urban resident an environment varied by the presence of nature, we are reducing his capacity to cope with change.

Cities are artifacts, conceived of by the mind of man, built by man, lived in by man. The experience of the city is in one sense incestuous. The sounds and sequences of nature, however, are different. Nature offers another kind of order—not inhuman, but most definitely non-human. And even if one were to prefer to live in the city, the experience of another kind of order would make a contribution to alertness and flexibility. Open space offers an opportunity for confrontation—not the confrontation of a new politics but a direct look into a system of which man is only a part. Open space

—natural open space—offers the setting for the discovery that all things affect each other. As we become ecologically aware, we inevitably become more humble, sensing that man is a part of nature, not versus nature, that we are indeed a part of a vast chain.

Aldo Leopold once wrote: "The problem we face is the extension of the social conscience from people to the land." When urban blacks talk of "community control," what they are trying to control is the decision-making community, not the ecological one. The notion of land as a community has little meaning for them. Confronted with the frustrations of trying to achieve a measure of autonomy over their lives, ghetto residents are attempting first to shape local school programs, to reduce hiring discrimination and to create more (and better) open housing. It is naive to assume that the urban black, burdened by enormous social and economic inequities, would place any priority on open space—on nature in the city.

Sometimes our talk of vest-pocket parks, open malls and riverfront promenades must seem like so much pie in the sky, at best pleasant, but unachievable. Yet we know that nature counts, not as an amenity, but as a vital ingredient in the mix that forms people who are healthy, capable of sustaining stress, flexible and adaptable to new situations. The urbanists say—understandably—that before we can achieve ecological solutions, we must first find solutions to the immediate problems of men. However, to wait for the advent of social nirvana while mankind's habitat is destroyed is no solution either. This is not a world which will permit us the luxury of solving our problems one at a time.

by Charles E. Little

Epilogue

In the back of our old farmhouse rises a big rock out-crop. It has a very special use. You climb up on the gentle side, near the barn; then, the rock breaks away sharply—a modest cliff, overlooking a wood and a shrub-swamp where ruffed grouse feed. You are about 30, 40 feet high, level with the tops of trees. You sit there, on the rock, and listen, and look at the woods and it is impossible, as Auden has put it, to rattle the cosmic slot machine of fate.

No one who goes to the rock (and we don't abuse the privilege) goes there to escape. When you sit on the edge, with your feet hanging down in the air, with the woods below you and all the bird and bug noises, you find you are not getting away from it all. You are getting *with it*. And you soon become aware that the rock has not, and most likely will not, ask to be justified. Nor will it justify you. You are just an organism that happens to be sitting on top of it. And sitting on top of it, you begin to wonder, "What can I do?"

Walt Kelly, the creator of Pogo, may just be the most quoted man in conservation circles since Henry David Thoreau. The environmental interpretation of "We have met the enemy, and he is us!" must be pretty

Charles E. Little, ex-adman and founder of the Open Space Institute, devotes full time now to writing and publishing in the environment field. He is the author of two books, including *Challenge of the Land*.

clear by now (unless you are reading this book backward). Well, that's a nice comfortable thought; I have yet to hear of the man who thought *us* was really *him*. Let's face it. To most of us, *us* is really *them*, for *them* is something you can really understand and lay righteous indignation on.

Around our neighborhood, which stands hard by the banks of the Hudson River, *them* is the Consolidated Edison Company. Due west are four of Con Ed's nuclear power plants. One of these plants at one time killed so many striped bass that they made a stinking pile as big as a freight car and had to be hauled away by truck under cover of darkness. And nobody yet knows anything about the effects of stray radiation. As an incipient grandparent, *I'd* like to know.

The high wires from this fish-killing plant slash across our local woodlands. More particularly, the unlovely spaghetti spans a nearby pond where my son and I go to fish for bass but get perch instead. At least Con Ed knows enough not to post this pond against fishermen. Any representative who showed up to kick people out would probably wind up in somebody's bait bucket.

Meanwhile, upstream, at Storm King Mountain, the utility still hopes to produce two units of power at peak periods of demand for every three expended in the process of pumping Hudson River water uphill into a cement lake. The objective of using up three units of power in order to supply two at a particular time, of course, is to avoid a power failure when all of *us* push our appliance plugs into *them* outlets.

The study in our old farmhouse overlooks four ancient and beautiful sugar maple trees, which we tapped once, and produced syrup at a cost of roughly $47 an ounce; the boiling-off process collapsed the kitchen ceiling. But we did not blame this on the trees. When it is too cold to sit outdoors on the rock, I sit in my study and look at the maples, making grim promises to myself to kill the next sonofabitch who does this or that to *my* environment. This is the way conservationists are. We believe there is this giant conspiracy, see. That the heads of Con Ed and Union Oil and the mayor, and for all we know, Spiro Agnew, get together periodically Cosa Nostra style in some mountain retreat to figure out how to murder the world. That's *them*. Right? And I am poor little *me*. Victim of environmental larceny. Parent and grandparent of victims unto the seventh generation, at which time, I can easily be convinced, horrible mutants will crawl weakly about the shrouded earth. And the mutants are telling each other that as far as Viet Nam is concerned, there is light at the end of the tunnel, that the corner has been turned, and that maybe we can spend more money now on environmental problems. The maple trees are long gone in this nightmare, never to pour their sweet juice into the ancient buckets, gone up the flue somewhere in a crabgrass factory.

So I am sitting in my study feeling persecuted, when from the street, along which our maples line up in stately splendor, I hear what Robert Frost described accurately as the snarl and rattle. Oh, God. I know that sound: *nraaaah, nraah, nraah, dip, dip, dippity, nraah, nraah.* It is like jackboots on the stairs at two A.M. and the pounding on the door. *'Raus, 'raus!* Like the booming howitzers closing on the city or the crashing of a thousand-year-old steeple on the street above the basement where we hide. *Nraah, nraah.* It is to me the sound of war. It is the *chainsaw.*

I leap up. My castered desk chair spins crazily out behind me, crashing into a bookcase which contains the incantations of Thoreau and Whitman, Krutch and Teale. I spin out of the study like a drag racer on Lake Muroc and I see *them:* the Con-Ed truck and a gaggle of goons standing around next to a motorized cherry picker whose elevated basket carries a workman with a chainsaw. He is lopping limbs off my maple trees as if they were so many banana bunches.

"What the hell are you doing?"

"Pruning your trees," says a man, who looks like he might be in charge. He is real loose: a pro. He does not look at me.

"Pruning my trees? *My* trees? My *trees!*"

"Pruning your trees," he replies evenly. He is absolutely in authority. They are in my tree. I am going out of my tree. Still he stands there. *Nraah, nraah.*

"Okay," I yell at him over the snarl and rattle. "Why are you pruning my trees?"

He tells me that they have to put an additional set of wires along the poles, which means they'll have to cross that bloody T again, now a double cross on the telephone poles. How many times crucified? Why hast thou forsaken my trees? He tells me this and a little hint of fatalism creeps into his voice, as if, after all, *he* did not like making crucifixes anymore than I. I have expended my anger. "What is it?" I ask mildly. "Another subdivision going in up the road? Is that why you need the new wires?"

He looks at me. Perhaps he senses my exhaustion, my weakness. "No subdivision," he says. "Just gadgets." And I turn, defeated, back to the old farmhouse with its electric toothbrushes, self-cleaning oven, drier and dishwasher and electric can-opener.

I have met the enemy.

And he is me.

Now I have this great vision of everybody going *straight,* starting with one guy who takes his goddamn electric toothbrush and stomps it to death right there on the bathroom floor. And he tells his girlfriend: "Look, I am going to knock you up exactly twice, and that's it. After that, zing. Vasectomy." And he goes to the car lot and asks the salesman how many horses are under the hood, and when the salesman says that she's got 472 cubes and 362 horses, the guy says: "Sorry, I wanted something like 75 horses. And keep your cubes to yourself."

Thus begins the process of consumption limitation.

It can happen. It happened before in periods of national emergency, most recently during World War II. In those days, kids learned how to flatten tin cans by taking out the end pieces, mashing them under foot and delivering 50 pounds in a little red wagon to the scrap metal depot, as part of the war effort. The Continental

Can Corporation could set up a similar program, as part of the peace-with-nature effort. Then Con-Can could fly the E flag. Remember the E flag? Only this time it would stand for ecology or environment. And in the windows of World War II hung the banners of the blue star families, with boys-at-arms overseas. Now we could have green star families if the old man gets his vasectomy and rides a bike to work instead of that 4,000 pound Super-Polluter Eight.

Remember defense stamps? We used to take a pocketful of change down to the post office and turn it into stamps to paste in our little book to save America. How about environment stamps? We could use the money to bond sewer districts and public works for pollution control, or to buy back those fine woods that should belong to everybody.

This is the kind of from-the-ground-up action that takes place in an emergency. It is the expression of *people,* doing their patriotic duty in individual ways.

I think that the U.S. survived World War II because it was a people's war. Everybody did his bit, from victory gardens to meatless Tuesdays. We knew exactly how to conserve our gasoline stamps by knowing exactly where to coast down a hill and where to re-start the engine on the way up. When wars are imposed from the top down, you don't win. If there is a lesson from the Sixties, that is it. But from the ground up, that's another matter, for it is the aggregate of individual actions that weighs the most in any emergency. This is why we have to start not with "them," not even with "us," but with *me.*

Back to the rock.

Presuming that I do go straight, ecologically speaking, I say to the rock—my great gray granite mentor in the back yard—then we'll still need some kind of cooperative action. I am reminded of that cartoon, dating, I think, from the Pleistocene, of two gents with their feet up on a desk. One says, "Next week we've got to get organized." After such a statement, one of two things is liable to happen. First, that they never will get organized, which is at least predictable. The second: they *will* get organized, which is infinitely worse, because from that point on organization will preclude any *possibility* of meaningful action. There is a kind of Gresham's law at work here: the processes of organization drive out creative action. Once Aldous Huxley said: "When a piece of work gets done in the world, who actually does it? Whose eyes and ears do the perceiving, whose cortex does the thinking, who has the feelings that motivate, the will that overcomes obstacles? Certainly not the social environment; for a group is not an organism, but only a blind unconscious organization. Everything that gets done within a society is done by individuals."

By and large, the real bell ringers in this environmental emergency turn out to be individuals, not organizations. There is no point in listing them, but two come to mind immediately in the area of persistent pesticides. The first was Rachel Carson with her book, *Silent Spring*. No need to explicate that text here. Miss Carson was before her time. So was Richard H. Pough, author of the *Audubon Bird Guides*, who, as resident ecologist at the National Audubon Society in 1945 B.C. (Before Carson) warned in the pages of the *New Yorker* of the effects of wholesale use of hard pesticides. It was the *New Yorker* that in 1962 serialized *Silent Spring*. But Pough, representing as he did this organization, got only about four inches of the Talk of the Town, his quote set forth with the slight smirk which is the hallmark (or was) of that magazine.

The most meaningful follow-through on the DDT crisis has been mounted by a young lawyer, Victor Yannacone, Jr., who brought actions against DDT in courts in New York and Wisconsin. Between Carson and Yannacone and a host of others playing less dramatic roles, the hard pesticides may be on the way out. The most important contributions to this happy state of affairs were *individual* contributions.

This is not to say that some cooperative structures aren't needed. They are needed as *media* for individual action. Thus, any new organizations should be started only after the possibilities of established one have been found wanting, and then only started on an ad hoc basis. (The same is true of laws. If all the time spent militating for some new law were instead spent bringing existing law to bear on an environmental problem, we'd be farther ahead. It is relevant to note that many of the civil rights cases have been won on the basis of the original civil rights act passed a century ago during the Reconstruction. Taking a page out of that book, Congressman Richard Ottinger of New York stopped the Penn Central Railroad from pollution practices by invoking a law that was passed in 1888.)

I find the view that "we've got to get organized" abhorrent. It postpones and dilutes the effort that must be made by each of us, the creative act that each of us must undertake, alone or in small groups. It is not enough for somebody to hand you a placard to carry, or a membership form to fill out. You have to *do* something.

I know a lady who lives in a ghetto of a small city. She works hard sewing curtains and slip covers. Her husband works hard in a VA Hospital, and comes home and reconstructs upholstered furniture and hangs the drapes that his wife makes. And they also manage to bring culture to their children because they are cultured people. One day the man and his wife looked across their street. They noticed the windows were broken in the houses there. The houses were poorly heated. They had too many families in them. They were owned by slum lords. And the children of the neighborhood were getting into trouble with the law. There was nothing for the children to do. So the man and his wife went to city hall and got nowhere. They went to the local churches and got nowhere. No one who was in a position to do something about the houses across the street would lift a finger.

So the man and his wife said to hell with the establishment, and they started saving their money. They began buying the houses. Six thousand for this one, eight thousand for that one. After about five years they owned a row of four houses. They fixed up the houses and tore down the fences in the back yards and put all the back yards together and graded the area. And now the kids have a place to play. Now they have trees and grass, a bit of honest, natural environment again because the man and the woman who made it happen didn't wait to get "organized."

So far the rock has transmitted two dangers to me. The first danger: confusing the so-called establishment with the real enemy—the individual who consumes the establishment's products. We have done without grapes for some time in our house. I suppose we could do without a lot of other things. More children, for instance.

The second is to be wary of the processes of organizations. Not of organizations themselves, but with the debilitating activities of "getting organized." Individual action against pollution, in defense of the environment, is a stronger weapon than most people realize. And it is the action that counts.

The final message from the outcrop has to do with *why*. So much of the time—and I have herein confessed to some of it myself—the environmentalist seems to be on some gigantic identity search. Not for the identity of the land, but for the identity of himself. If there is anything that the rock teaches it is not to confuse the two. Why bother with the environment? Because you are sore at Con Ed? That surely cannot be the basic motivation. For posterity? That sounds a little better, but has become so much a part of the ecological rhetoric that it sounds suspicious. I am sure that my great grandchildren will all be fine citizens, good looking and happy. But I won't know them.

What is it, then, that drives us? What is it that *really* gets us concerned, under all the journalism of ecology and the jeremiads of the biological scientists? It just can't be some kind of intellectual exercise, or the whole movement is doomed to fail. It is, I think, based on something deep within us, the spiritual atom that makes us persist in surviving, that makes us believe in the dignity of the land itself. It is translated into what I can only call "land love." I believe we all possess land love. Some let it surface, and we call them conservationists. And I guess I am one. But for me, land love had been relatively latent until I took my family on an eight thousand mile motor tour of the United States. Among other things, we learned what the expression "big sky" really meant. We went through a blizzard at 12,000 feet down a desert floor with temperatures nearing a hundred (it was cool). We saw soaring buttes, the great canyon gashes—the Green, the Colorado; the Pacific from atop Mt. Tamalpais; the scurrying lizards in the Southwest; a mighty thunderstorm in Texas. Big sky, big land.

One night we stayed in Carson City, and since the family is hooked on enchiladas, tacos and refried beans, I stopped at a phone booth to look at the yellow pages for a Mexican restaurant. The book I found was about the size of the directory we have in our office for Danbury, Connecticut. It took me a few minutes to discover that the one in Carson City covered the entire state of Nevada.

If the gas station attendant near Zuni, New Mexico, had asked me what I did for a living, I'm not sure that I could have answered him in less than ten thousand words, plus a portfolio of photographs. As it was, he said, "Nice day."

"Helluva nice day," I said.

"Nice day to go fishin'," he said.

"Where do you go?" I asked, looking at the dry landscape beyond the cottonwoods at his crossroads.

"Up to the new reservoir."

"Whaddya get?" I affected the merest southwestern drawl.

"Oh, bream, catfish, trout." And I thought, here is this man two thousand, no, better than two thousand miles away from where I live, and I suspect we could've spent the rest of the afternoon talking about fishing.

Earlier that day we talked with an Indian man. "I am a Zuni. I married a Laguna." And he narrowed his eyes. "Hahn," he grunted, implicating us in this radical contract with the daughter of a distant tribe.

He told us where to find the pueblo of his wife's people. It was perched on a bluff above U.S. 66 and behind it stretched the arid flats and technicolor escarpments of the desert beyond sight and beyond ken. The children of the union of Zuni and Laguna could know that there had been other unions back in time to the old ones—the Anasazi—who even then lived in pueblos, and who had seen the mountains spurt fire and the hot red stream that this day we scrambled over: the weathered, lichened black lava flow. All of us were, for a time, from the big land.

It is a hallowing thought—knowing that you are a part of this vastness, all strange, all familiar. It is a thought that comes to people like me and my family rarely, to millions not at all. When you return to the city there are two kinds of constructions you can put on such an experience—the big sky, the big land, the settlement so thin that it can be recorded in a phone book no thicker than three-eighths of an inch.

One is that there is so much space *there* that our zealousness here, in the city and its environs, to save the little woods remaining, and streams and ponds is somehow absurd.

But I prefer the other view, that America *is* the land, and that we are of it: I no less than the Zuni, my wife no less than the Laguna. The gas station man and I are fishermen together wherever we live. All the children of all our families should prowl the deserts, tracking horned toads, or the woods and ponds searching for frogs and red efts.

The land. There is magic in it, and strength.

appendix

The appendix for *ecotactics* was compiled by Connie Flateboe, Vivian Lewin and Robert Waldrop of the Sierra Club staff; Club volunteers Nancy Mathews and Hilde Werthauer, and Mary Jefferds of the National Audubon Society's Bay Area Educational Services.

THE ACTIVIST'S CHECKLIST

√ Don't buy beverages in *one-way* ("no deposit, no return") containers; save the two-way bottles and return them to the store. Use as little tinfoil and plastic wrap as possible. They are non-biodegradable. Save six-packs of empty one-way containers and ship them back to the board of directors of the company that manufactured the product. Tell them that you are tired of "no deposit-no return."

√ Save water. Put bricks in the tank of your toilet so it uses less water when flushed. Don't leave the faucet on while you're brushing your teeth.

√ Avoid using electrical appliances, especially dish-washers, in the evening "prime" hours (5 to 7 P.M.). This is "peaking power" time, and your participation in it justifies many Bureau of Reclamation and municipal utility claims that more dams or other power facilities are needed. Do you really need an electric toothbrush? An electric can opener? An electric carving knife? Whatever happened to *muscle*-power?

√ Consume less. If we begin by reducing our personal over-consumption, we may, one day, begin to live in harmony with the land.

√ Find a dirty hillside, creek, canyon, beach, or

roadside. (You won't have to look far.) Tell the land-owner you're going to clean it up. Call the (under-ground/above ground) newspapers, TV, radio, and tell them what you're doing. Call the city refuse collection department. Ask how to recycle the various types of waste you expect to collect. If it can't be recycled, why not? If it can, separate the garbage into piles of paper, glass, aluminum or tin cans, plastic, scrap iron, etc. Are any of the containers returnable? Why not? Where does the refuse collection department take the solid waste materials *it* picks up? Where does this waste wind up? In the air above an incinerator, or buried in a marsh?

√ Look at your community's lakes, ponds and water-courses. How polluted are they? Can you drink from them? Can fish live in them? Can you swim in them, or use them for recreation of any kind? Ask the local office of the Federal Water Pollution Control Administration (Department of the Interior) about its standards for water quality. What is it doing—specifically—to control pollution? Is it enough? What pollutes the water locally —factories, sewage treatment plants, agricultural run-off? Locate your sewage disposal plant and ask for evidence of its efficiency. How much untreated water each week goes back into the water supply? What happens to the sanitary sewers when it rains? Write your state de-partment of health or water quality board and request sterile sample bottles and directions for testing the qual-ity of ponds and streams. No bottles, no directions? Why not?

√ Consider the air. Does it smell bad? Does it fog the view? Ask the local air pollution control agency what its standards are for air quality. How well is it able to enforce them? Does the state have stronger or weaker standards, or none at all? Report observable violators (smokestacks, transit systems, etc.). Be specific.

√ Do you have a favorite haunt or campsite in a na-tional park, on a wild riverbank, on an ocean or lake beach, high mountain pass, grassy meadow? Are there plans for its "improvement"? Find out from the tax office of the county in which it is located who is responsible for its administration—private owner, National Park Service, U.S. Forest Service, Bureau of Land Management, state or federal fish and game agency. If development plans exist, what are the administering agency's standards? Do they provide adequate safeguards? What do *you* think should be done in the area, if anything?

√ Does your town, county or region have an inventory of open space lands? Why not? Is there a vacant lot in your neighborhood that could be made into a park or recreation area? Find out from the county tax assessor's office what the plans are for its disposition. How many downtown outdoor parking lots are scheduled to have high-rise office or apartment buildings constructed on them? What will this construction do to the city's density, services, "tax base"? Does your county council or board of supervisors know why open space in the inner city is so essential? Maybe not. Educate them.

THE ACTIVIST'S BOOKSHELF:
A BIBLIOGRAPHY

Environment: General

Dasmann, Raymond F. *The Destruction of California*. (New York: 1965). Macmillan.

Douglas, William O. *Wilderness Bill of Rights*. (Boston: 1965). Little, Brown. 5.95; pap. 1.95.

Marine, Gene. *America The Raped*. (New York: 1969). Simon & Schuster. 5.95.

Marx, Wesley. *The Frail Ocean*. (New York: 1967). Coward-McCann. 5.95; Sierra Club and Ballantine Books. pap. .95.

National Academy of Sciences, Committee on Resources, *Resources and Man*. (San Francisco: 1969). National Research Council; W. H. Freeman.

Osborn, Robert. *Mankind May Never Make It!* (New York: 1968). New York Graphic Society. 5.95; pap. 2.50.

President's Council on Recreation and Natural Beauty. *From Sea to Shining Sea, A Report on the American Environment —Our Natural Heritage*. (Washington, D.C.: 1968). Superintendent of Documents, Government Printing Office. pap. 2.50.

Rienow, Robert and Leona Train. *Moment in the Sun*. (New York: 1969). Sierra Club and Ballantine Books. .95.

Stewart, George Ripley. *Not so Rich as You Think*. (Boston: 1968). Houghton Mifflin. 5.00.

Udall, Stewart. *1976: Agenda for Tomorrow*. (New York: 1969). Holt, Rinehart and Winston. 3.75.

Environment: Anthologies and Symposia

Adams, R. M., et al. *The Fitness of Man's Environment*. (New York: 1967). Smithsonian Institution and Random House. 5.95.

Cox, George W., ed. *Readings in Conservation Ecology*. (New York, 1969). Appleton-Century-Crofts. 4.95.

Darling, Frank Fraser, and John P. Milton, eds. *Future Environments of North America: Transformation of a Continent*. (Garden City, N.Y.: 1966). Natural History Press. 12.50.

Ewald, William R., Jr., ed. *Environment and Change: The Next Fifty Years*. (Bloomington: 1968). Indiana University Press. 10.00; pap. 4.95.

_____, ed. *Environment and Policy: The Next Fifty Years*. (Bloomington: 1968). Indiana University Press. 10.00; pap. 4.95.

_____, ed. *Environment For Man: The Next Fifty Years*. (Bloomington: 1967). Indiana University Press. 6.95; pap. 2.95.

Graubard, Stephen R., ed. "America's Changing Environment" in *Daedalus*, Fall, 1967. American Academy of Arts and Sciences.

Shepard, Paul, and Daniel McKinley, eds. *The Subversive Science: Essays Toward An Ecology of Man*. (Boston: 1969). Houghton Mifflin. 8.95; pap. 5.95.

Eco-Philosophy

Abbey, Edward. *Desert Solitaire: A Season in the Wilderness*. (New York: 1968). McGraw-Hill. 5.95.

Beston, Henry. *The Outermost House*. (New York: 1969). The Viking Compass. pap. 1.45.

Dubos, René. *So Human An Animal*. (New York: 1970). Charles Scribner's Sons. 6.95; pap. 2.25.

Edberg, Rolf. *On The Shred of a Cloud.* Sven Ahman, trans. (Alabama: 1969). University of Alabama Press. 6.50.

Leopold, Aldo A. *A Sand Country Almanac and Sketches Here and There.* (New York: 1968). Oxford University Press. pap. 1.75.

Russell, Jerry, and Renny Russell. *On The Loose.* (New York: 1969). Sierra Club and Ballantine Books. pap. 3.95.

Thoreau, Henry David. *Walden.* (Many editions available.)

Ecology and Natural History

Bates, Marston. *The Forest and the Sea: A Look at the Economy of Nature and the Ecology of Man.* (New York: 1960). Random House. 4.95; pap. 1.65.

Boom, B. K. and H. Kleijn. *The Glory of the Tree.* (New York: 1966). Doubleday and Company. 12.95.

Farb, Peter. *Ecology.* (New York: 1963). Time-Life Books. 6.60.

Farb, Peter. *Face of North America: The Natural History of a Continent.* (New York: 1968). Harper & Row, Colophon Book. pap. 1.95.

Feininger, Andreas. *Trees.* (New York: 1968). Viking Press. 22.50.

Kormondy, Edward J. *Concepts of Ecology.* (New York: 1969). Prentice-Hall. 4.95; pap. 2.95.

Krutch, Joseph Wood. *The Great Chain of Life.* (Boston: 1957). Houghton Mifflin. 4.50.

Levins, Richard. *Evolution in Changing Environments: Some Theoretical Explanations.* (Princeton: 1968). Princeton University Press. 6.50; pap. 3.95.

Odum, Eugene P. *Ecology.* (New York: 1963). Holt, Rinehart and Winston. pap. 3.25.

Platt, Rutherford. *The Great American Forest.* (Englewood Cliffs: 1965). Prentice-Hall. 7.95.

Raskin, Edith. *Pyramid of Living Things.* (New York: 1967). McGraw-Hill. 4.00.

Sears, Paul B. *Lands Beyond the Forest.* (Englewood Cliffs: 1968). Prentice-Hall. 7.95.

Smith, Robert. *Ecology and Field Biology.* (New York: 1966). Harper & Row. 13.95.

Science of Pollution

A National Policy for the Environment. A Special Report to the Committee on Interior and Insular Affairs, U.S. Senate, July 11, 1968. (Request from Committee Chairman, U.S. Senate, Washington, D.C. 20510.)

American Chemical Society Report. *Cleaning Our Environment: The Chemical Basis for Action.* (Washington, D.C.: 1969). American Chemical Society. 2.75.

Carson, Rachel. *Silent Spring.* (Boston: 1962). Houghton Mifflin. 5.95. Fawcett World. pap. .95.

Commoner, Barry. *Science and Survival.* (New York: 1968). Viking Compass. 4.50; pap. 1.35.

Edelson, Edward, and Fred Warshofsky. *Poisons in the Air.* (New York: 1966). Pocket Books. 1.00.

Environmental Quality. Hearings before the Subcommittee on Science, Research, and Development of the Committee on Science and Astronautics, U.S. House of Representatives, 90th Congress, 2nd Session. (Request from Committee Chairman, address U.S. House of Representatives, Washington, D.C., 20515.)

Goldstein, Jerome. *Garbage As You Like It.* (Emmaus, Pa.: 1969). Rodale Books.

Hersh, Seymour M. *Chemical and Biological Warfare: America's Hidden Arsenal.* (Garden City, N.Y.: 1969). Doubleday. pap. 1.45.

Joint House-Senate Colloquium To Discuss A National Policy for the Environment. Hearing before the Committee of Interior and Insular Affairs, U.S. Senate, and Committee on Science and Astronautics, House. 90th Congress, 2nd Session, July 17, 1968. (Request from either Committee Chairman.)

Leinwand, Gerald, gen. ed. *Air and Water Pollution.* (New York: 1969). Washington Square Press. pap. .75.

Managing the Environment. Report of the Subcommittee on Science, Research, and Development to the Committee on Science and Astronautics, U.S. House of Representatives. 1968.

National Academy of Sciences, *Ad Hoc* Panel on Technology Assessment. *Technology: Processes of Assessment and Choice.* 1969. (Prepared for Committee on Science and Astronautics, U.S. House of Representatives.) Government Printing Office. .75.

President's Science Advisory Committee, Environmental Pollution Panel. *Restoring the Quality of Our Environment.* (Washington, D.C.: 1965). Government Printing Office. 1.25.

Rudd, Robert L. *Pesticides and the Living Landscape.* (Madison: 1964). University of Wisconsin Press. pap. 1.95.

Shurcliff, William A. *SST and Sonic Boom Handbook.* (New York: 1970). Friends of the Earth and Ballantine Books. .95.

U.S. Dept. of Health, Education and Welfare, Public Health Service. *Take Three Giant Steps to Clean Air.* (Washington, D.C.: 1966). Government Printing Office.

U.S. Dept. of Health, Education and Welfare, Public Health Service. *The Effects of Air Pollution.* (Washington, D.C.: 1967). Government Printing Office.

U.S. Dept. of Health, Education and Welfare, Task Force on Environmental Health and Related Problems. *A Strategy for a Livable Environment.* (Washington, D.C.: 1967). Government Printing Office. .60.

Open Space and the Urban Environment

Chermayeff, Serge, and Christopher Alexander. *Community and Privacy: Toward a New Architecture of Humanism.* (New York: 1963). Doubleday. 5.95; pap. 1.75.

Eckbo, Garrett. *Urban Landscape Design.* (New York: 1964). McGraw-Hill. 16.50.

Federal Highway Administrator's Urban Advisors. *The Freeway in the City.* (Washington, D.C.: 1968). Government Printing Office.

Jacobs, Jane. *The Death and Life of Great American Cities.* (New York: 1961). Random House. 7.95; Modern Library, 2.45; pap. 1.95.

Little, Charles E. *Challenge of the Land.* (New York: 1969). Pergamon Press. 3.75.

McHarg, Ian. *Design with Nature.* (Garden City: 1969). Natural History Press. 19.95.

Mowbray, A. Q. *The Road to Ruin.* (Philadelphia and New York: 1969). J. B. Lippincott. 5.95.

Norcross, Carl. *Open Space Communities in the Marketplace.* (Washington D.C.: 1966). Urban Land Institute.

Seymour, Whitney North, Jr., ed. *Small Urban Spaces.* (New York: 1969). New York University Press. 6.50.

Vosburgh, John. *Living with Your Land.* (Bloomfield Hills, Mich.: 1968). Cranbrook Institute of Science.

Whyte, William H. *The Last Landscape.* (New York: 1968). Doubleday. 6.50.

Population

Borgstrom, Georg. *The Hungry Planet.* (New York: 1965). MacMillan. 7.95; pap. 2.95.

Calderone, Mary Steichen, ed. *Manual of Contraceptive Practice.* (Baltimore: 1963). Williams and Wilkins.

Ehrlich, Paul. *The Population Bomb.* (New York: 1969). Sierra Club and Ballantine Books. pap. .95.

Guttmacher, Alan F. *Complete Book of Birth Control.* (New York). Ballantine. .50.

Hardin, Garrett, ed. *Population, Evolution and Birth Control.* (San Francisco: 1969). W. H. Freeman & Co. 6.00; pap. 2.95.

Himes, Norman E., and Abraham Stone, M.D. *Planned Parenthood: A Practical Guide to Birth Control Methods.* (New York: 1965). Collier. .95.

Paddock, William, and Paul Paddock. *Famine—1975!* (Boston: 1967). Little, Brown. 6.50; pap. 2.35.

Young, Louise B. *Population in Perspective.* (New York: 1968). Oxford University Press. 10.00; pap. 4.95.

Wilderness and Wildlife

Brooks, Paul. *Roadless Area.* (New York: 1969). Alfred A. Knopf. 4.95.

Brower, David, ed. *The Meaning of Wilderness to Science.* (New York: 1960). Sierra Club. 5.95.

—————, ed. *Wilderness: America's Living Heritage.* (New York: 1961). Sierra Club. 5.95.

—————, ed. *Wildlands in Our Civilization.* (New York: 1964). Sierra Club. 5.95.

Fisher, James; Noel Simon and Jack Vincent. *Wildlife in Danger.* (New York: 1968). Viking Press. 12.95.

Kilgore, Bruce, ed. *Wilderness in a Changing World.* (New York: 1966). Sierra Club. 6.50.

Leydet, Francois, ed. *Tomorrow's Wilderness.* (New York: 1963). Sierra Club. 5.95.

Matthiessen, Peter. *Wildlife in North America.* (New York: 1959). Viking Press. 6.00; pap. 1.95.

McCloskey, Maxine and James P. Gilligan, eds. *Wilderness and the Quality of Life.* (New York: 1969). Sierra Club. 6.50.

Nash, Roderick. *Wilderness and the American Mind.* (New Haven: 1967). Yale University Press. 6.50.

A ROSTER OF ROUND EARTH SOCIETIES

There are still those who insist that the earth is flat, or at least their thought processes wander flatly in that direction. These are the people who think in straight lines, as if the earth and all its resources were infinite. Circles horrify them. And the very idea of the earth as a closed system is so horribly circular it's enough to send them screaming up a nice, friendly, flat wall.

But wise men are not so square. They believe in a round earth and all that a round earth implies. And in these United States, millions are backing up that belief by joining or supporting the "round earth societies," the conservation and environmental organizations which, in one way or another, are contributing to the cause of man's survival on this round planet.

Here is a roster of some of those societies:

American Forestry Association, 919 17th St. N.W., Washington, D.C. 20006. Private organization promoting conservation of forests and associated resources. Publishes *American Forests,* monthly magazine.

Appalachian Trail Conference, 1718 N Street N.W., Washington, D.C. 20036. Coordinates maintenance of the AT, Maine to Georgia. Can provide trail guidance for new trail groups.

California Roadside Council, 2626 Ocean Avenue, San Francisco, California 94132. Statewide citizens' organization promoting natural beauty, billboard control, and undergrounding of utilities.

California Tomorrow, Monadnock Building, 681 Market Street, San Francisco, California 94105. Fosters educational awareness of California conservation problems. Publishes *Cry California,* quarterly magazine.

Citizens for Clean Air, 40 W. 57th Street, New York, N.Y. 10019. Private organization promoting action for cleaner air. Posters.

Citizens League against the Sonic Boom, 19 Appleton Street, Cambridge, Massachusetts 02138. Just what it says.

Colorado Open Space Council, 5850 E. Jewell Avenue, Denver, Colorado 80222. Statewide federation of citizens' organizations coordinating action in preservation and wise use of open space.

Conservation Education Association, 1250 Connecticut Avenue N.W., Washington, D.C. 20036. Fosters conservation education programs in public schools, and training of teachers. Newsletter, bibliography, reports, etc.

Conservation Foundation, 1250 Connecticut Avenue N.W., Washington, D.C. Privately supported organization for research, information, education. Publishes a monthly newsletter.

Conservation Law Society of America, Mills Tower, 220 Bush Street, San Francisco, California 94104. On fee basis, counsels litigants in cases of nationwide importance.

Defenders of Wildlife, 1346 Connecticut Avenue N.W., Washington, D.C. 20036. And that's what they are.

Desert Protective Council, P.O. Box 33, Banning, California 92220. Safeguards important desert areas.

Ducks, Unlimited, P.O. Box 66300, Chicago, Illinois 60666. Promotes and assists conservation of wild waterfowl habitats in U.S. and Canada.

Federation of Western Outdoor Clubs, c/o Betty Hughes, Route 3, Box 172, Carmel, California 93921. Promotes proper use, protection and enjoyment of outdoor resources for its 44 member organizations.

Friends of the Earth, 451 Pacific Avenue, San Francisco 94133. An international conservation organization. Very new, but very aggressive.

Garden Clubs of America, 598 Madison Avenue, New York, N.Y. 10022. Organization of local clubs promoting horticulture, natural resource conservation, landscaping. Provides information on pending legislation. Scholarships. Educational material for teachers.

International Shade Tree Conference, 1827 Neil Avenue, Columbus, Ohio 43210. Promotes better planting and preservation of shade trees. Film and slides presentations. *Arborist News,* monthly. Publishes papers on specific problems.

Izaak Walton League of America, 1326 Waukegan Road, Glenview, Illinois 60025. Membership organization with many chapters and state divisions. Not just for fishermen. Speakers, literature, monthly newspaper, educational materials.

Massachusetts Audubon Society, South Great Road, Lincoln, Massachusetts 01776. Separate entity from national society. Innovative in conservation communications.

National Association of Soil and Water Conservation Districts, 1025 Vermont Avenue N.W., Washington, D.C. 20005. Several thousand local districts conserving natural resources. Advisory committee for private landowners.

National Audubon Society, 1130 Fifth Avenue, New York, N.Y. 10038. Membership organization; numerous state chapters and representatives. Programs for youngsters. Technical assistance in setting up nature centers. Field assistance at cost. Publishes *Audubon,* excellent bimonthly magazine, teaching aids, bulletins, manuals, other publications. Furnishes films and speakers.

National Council of State Garden Clubs, 4401 Magnolia Avenue, St. Louis, Missouri 63110. Nationwide organization of local clubs. Furnishes filmstrips and films.

National Parks Association, 1701 18th Street N.W., Washington, D.C. 20009. Protects national park system and other natural environments. Monthly *National Parks* magazine. Leaflets for school use.

National Recreation and Park Association, 1700 Pennsylvania Avenue N.W., Washington, D.C. 20006. Publishes monthly *Parks and Recreation* magazine, newsletters; public information programs and research services.

National Trust for Historic Preservation, Decatur House, 748 Jackson Place N.W., Washington, D.C. 20006. Advice and technical assistance on preservation of sites significant in U.S. history. Maintains some properties for public. Leaflets on preservation law and restoration, quarterly journal, monthly newspaper.

National Wildlife Federation, 1412 16th Street N.W., Washington, D.C. Encourages wise use and management of natural resources. Graduate student grants. Informational material for media. Publishes bimonthly *National Wildlife* Magazine, newsletters, booklets.

The Nature Conservancy, 1522 K Street N.W., Washington, D.C. Acquires threatened land through revolving loan fund. Manages system of reserves. Provides technical and financial assistance to landowners. Publishes quarterly *News* and pamphlets.

Open Space Institute, 145 East 52nd Street, New York, N.Y. 10022. Professional consultants advise municipalities, corporations and private landowners in open space preservation priorities and techniques. Books and technical reports available.

Open Lands Project, 123 W. Madison Street, Chicago, Illinois 60602. Pushes for action to save threatened areas in Chicago area.

Planned Parenthood, 515 Madison Avenue, New York, N.Y. 10022. For fewer babies, obviously.

Regional Plan Association, 230 W. 41st Street, New York, N.Y. 10036. Organization concerned with intelligent development of N.Y., N.J. and Connecticut. Annual conference. Research bulletins and periodicals.

Resources for the Future, 1145 19th Street N.W., Washington, D.C. 20006. Education and research into wise use of natural resources. Grants. Reports. A storehouse of statistics.

Save-the-Redwoods League, 114 Sansome Street, San Francisco, California 94104. Preserving those big trees.

Sierra Club (see separate Appendix listing).

Sport Fishing Institute, 719 13th Street N.W., Washington, D.C. 20005. More fish. Research. Education.

Trout Unlimited, 2526 State Street, P.O. Box 1807, Saginaw, Michigan. 48605. Membership organization formed to preserve clear water and to improve quality of fishing by supporting high regulative standards and research.

Urban America, 1717 Massachusetts Avenue N.W., Washington, D.C. 20036. Promotes best use of urban lands. Publishes bimonthly, *City*. Brochures.

Western Pennsylvania Conservancy, 204 Fifth Avenue, Pittsburgh, Pennsylvania 15222. Large and active state organization for acquisition of parks, nature centers, historic landmarks. Speakers bureau, educational program.

The Wilderness Society, 729 15th Street N.W., Washington, D.C. 20005. To defend and to increase knowledge of wilderness. Quarterly magazine, *The Living Wilderness*.

PROFESSIONAL GROUPS AND SOCIETIES

American Association for the Advancement of Science
1515 Massachusetts Avenue N.W.
Washington, D.C. 20005

American Association of Botanical Gardens and Arboretums
c/o Francis DeVos
Chicago Botanical Garden
116 South Michigan Avenue
Chicago, Illinois 60603

American Association of Interpretive Naturalists
1251 East Broad Street
Columbus, Ohio 43205

American Association of Zoological Parks and Aquariums
Oglebay Park
Wheeling, West Virginia 26003

American Institute of Architects
1735 New York Avenue, N.W.
Washington, D.C. 20006

American Institute of Biological Sciences
3900 Wisconsin Avenue, N.W.
Washington, D.C. 20016

American Institute of Planners
917 15th Street, N.W.
Room 800
Washington, D.C. 20005

American Littoral Society
Sandy Hook
Highlands, New Jersey 07732

American Museum Association
Smithsonian Institution
Washington, D.C. 20020

American Nature Study Society
c/o William Stapp
1501 Granada
Ann Arbor, Michigan 48103

American Ornithologists' Union
c/o John Aldrich
Bureau of Sport Fisheries and Wildlife
U.S. Department of the Interior
Washington, D.C. 20240

American Planning and Civic Association
901 Union Trust Building
Washington, D.C. 20005

American Society for Range Management
2120 South Birch Street
Denver, Colorado 80222

American Society of Agronomy
677 Segoe Road
Madison, Wisconsin 53711

American Society of Ichthyologists and Herpetologists
c/o Charles Walker
Museum of Zoology
University of Michigan
Ann Arbor, Michigan 48104

American Society of Landscape Architects
2013 Eye Street N.W.
Washington, D.C. 20006

American Society of Limnology and Oceanography
c/o F. Ronald Hayes
Fisheries Research Board of Canada
Ottawa, Ontario, Canada

American Society of Mammalogists
c/o Richard Van Gelder
American Museum of Natural History
Central Park W. at 79th St.
New York, New York 10024

American Society of Planning Officials
1313 E. 60th Street
Chicago, Illinois 60637

Association of American Geographers
1146 16th Street N.W.
Washington, D.C. 20036

Association of Conservation Engineers
c/o Don Hays
Department of Fish and Wildlife Resources
State Office Building Annex
Frankfort, Kentucky 40601

Association of Consulting Foresters
Box 6
Wake, Virginia 23176

Ecological Society of America
c/o John Cantlon
Department of Botany
Michigan State University
East Lansing, Michigan 48823

National Academy of Sciences
2101 Constitution Ave., N.W.
Washington, D.C.

National Science for Youth Foundation
114 East 30th Street
New York, New York 10016

National Speleological Society
203 Virginia Hills Avenue
Alexandria, Virginia

Outdoor Writers' Association of America
Outdoors Building
Columbia, Missouri 65201

Scientists' Institute for Public Information
30 East 68th Street
New York, New York 10021
(A *great* reservoir of information.)

Society of American Foresters
1010 16th Street, N.W.
Washington, D.C.

Soil Conservation Society of America
835 - 5th
Des Moines, Iowa 50309

The Wildlife Society
3900 Wisconsin Avenue, N.W.
Washington, D.C. 20016

CONGRESSIONAL DIRECTORY

STRATEGIC COMMITTEES AND SUBCOMMITTEES OF THE HOUSE

Committee on Agriculture
W. R. Poage (D.-Texas)

Subcommittee on Forests
John L. McMillan (D.-S. Car.)

Committee on Appropriations
George H. Mahon (D.-Texas)

Subcommittee on Interior and Related Agencies
Julia Butler Hansen (D.-Wash.)

Subcommittee on Public Works
Michael J. Kirwan (D.-Ohio)

Committee on Government Operations
William L. Dawson (D.-Ill.)

Subcommittee on Conservation and Natural Resources
Henry Reuss (D.-Wis.)

Committee on Interior and Insular Affairs
Wayne N. Aspinall (D.-Colo.)

Subcommittee on Indian Affairs
James A. Haley (D.-Fla.)

Subcommittee on National Parks and Recreation
Roy A. Taylor (D.-N. Car.)

Subcommittee on Public Lands
Walter S. Baring (D.-Nev.)

Committee on Merchant Marine and Fisheries
Edward A. Garmatz (D.-Md.)

Subcommittee on Fisheries and Wildlife Conservation
John D. Dingell (D.-Mich.)

Committee on Public Works
George H. Fallon (D.-Md.)

Subcommittee on Rivers and Harbors
John A. Blatnik (D.-Minn.)

Subcommittee on Roads
John C. Kluczynski (D.-Ill.)

STRATEGIC COMMITTEES AND SUBCOMMITTEES OF THE SENATE

Committee on Agriculture and Forestry
Allen J. Ellender (D.-La.)

Subcommittee on Soil Conservation and Forestry
James O. Eastland (D.-Miss.)

Committee on Appropriations
Richard B. Russell (D.-Ga.)

Subcommittee on Department of Interior and Related Agencies
Alan Bible (D.-Nev.)

Subcommittee on Public Works
Allen J. Ellender (D.-La.)

Committee on Commerce
Warren G. Maguson (D.-Wash.)

Subcommittee on Energy, Natural Resources, and the Environment
Philip A. Hart (D.-Mich.)

Committee on Interior and Insular Affairs
Henry M. Jackson (D.-Wash.)

Subcommittee on Indian Affairs
George McGovern (S. Dakota)

Subcommittee on Parks and Recreation
Alan Bible (D.-Nev.)

Committee on Public Works
Jennings Randolph (D.-W. Va.)

Subcommittee on Air and Water Pollution
Edmund S. Muskie (D.-Maine)

Subcommittee on Flood Control-River and Harbors
Stephen M. Young (D.-Ohio)

Subcommittee on Public Roads
Jennings Randolph (D.-W. Va.)

KEY FEDERAL AGENCIES

Department of Agriculture

Agricultural Stablization and Conservation Service—Gives financial assistance to farmers who convert cropland to open space for natural habitat or recreation use. Shares cost of implementing conservation practices with farmers.

Federal Extension Service—Education programs and field agents help development of resources, conservation practices and recreational use.

Forest Service—Manages National Forests and grasslands. Offers technical and financial aid and research to landowners for forest and wildlife management.

Soil Conservation Service—Works with local water and soil conservation districts to provide technical assistance in planning and implementing local projects. Conducts soil surveys, publishes basic water conservation and land use data.

Department of Commerce

Business and Defense Services Administration—Consults with business on industrial problems including air, water and waste pollution.

Department of Health, Education and Welfare

National Center for Air Pollution Control—offers grants, technical assistance, personnel training for air pollution control programs, agencies, studies, private agencies.

Office of Education—curriculum development and innovative center grants for local school systems. Grants for adult education on community problems such as urban planning and conservation.

National Center for Urban and Industrial Health—office of Solid Waste: research in waste disposal methods and controls. Environmental Sanitation Program: technical assistance and standards development for recreational areas, housing hygiene, urban noise and crowding; conducts and supports research and training.

Department of Housing and Urban Development

Land and Facilities Development Administration—open Space Land Program helps fund acquisition and preservation of open space land for public conservation and recreational uses.

Office of Urban Studies and Clearinghouse Services—studies housing and other urban problems including open space and urban land improvement projects.

Department of the Interior

Bureau of Commercial Fisheries—researches management and conservation of key marine and inland fishery resources. Offers grants, loans, technical aid.

Bureau of Indian Affairs.

Bureau of Land Management—manages Federally-owned lands (500 million acres, mainly in the West), makes public domain lands available for lease or purchase for environmental improvement purposes. Conducts studies on urban open space planning, highway planning.

Bureau of Mines—research and development, and conservation of mineral resources; develops model control regulations; advises local and state air groups; studies air and water pollution problems related to mineral use.

Bureau of Outdoor Recreation—helps coordinate Federal plans and programs in outdoor recreation areas. Technical aid available to state, local and private interests in developing outdoor recreation resources.

Bureau of Reclamation—planning, construction and operation of water resource programs in the West. Builder of dams—many unneeded.

Bureau of Sport Fisheries and Wildlife—works with state agencies to manage fish and wildlife resources. Manages National Wildlife Refuges and fish hatcheries; is responsible for migratory birds and rare and endangered species. Research and technical assistance available.

Federal Water Pollution Control Administration—reviews state water quality standards, carries out interstate enforcement activities, financial aid for municipal waste treatment projects; grants for river basin planning programs, and interstate pollution control agencies.

Geological Survey—conducts mapping, research on mineral resources and geologic structure and on water and sediment flow above and underground.

National Park Service—planning, development and management of the National Park System. Includes information and interpretive services.

Office of Water Resources Research—coordinates research and promotes information exchange; offers financial aid programs for research and training in water resources field.

National Science Foundation

Research activities include basic study of environmental programs.

Water Resources Council

Inter-departmental agency, establishes river basin commissions for key areas to coordinate plans on all government levels for water and land resources. Financial aid to states in developing comprehensive water and related land resources programs.

SIERRA CLUB DIRECTORY

Head office:
1050 Mills Tower
San Francisco, California
   94104
(415) 981-8634

   Executive Director
   California Representative
   Campus Representative
   Forestry Consultant
   News Editor
   Membership Department
   Outing Department
   Sales Manager
   Sierra Club Bulletin

Los Angeles office:
430 Auditorium Building
427 West Fifth Street
Los Angeles, California 90013
(213) 622-1885

Atlantic office:
250 West 57th Street
New York, New York 10019
(212) 265-2818

Washington office:
235 Massachusetts Ave. N.E.
Washington, D.C. 20002
(202) 547-1144

Southwest office:
2014 East Broadway
Room 16
Tucson, Arizona 85719
(602) 623-2048

Northwest office:
4534½ University Way NE
Seattle, Washington 98105
(206) 632-6157

Alaska office:
Box 5-425
College, Alaska 99701

CHAPTERS AND GROUPS

Alaska

Gerald Ganopole, Chairman
2536 Arlington Drive
Anchorage, Alaska 99503

Theodore Dunn, Conservation
  Chairman
429 D Street—Suite 201
Anchorage, Alaska 99501

Fairbanks Group
Gordon Wright
Box 5-051
College, Alaska 99701

Juneau Group
Dr. Donald Freedman
Box 1427
Juneau, Alaska 99801

Sitka Group
Dr. George H. Longenbaugh
Box 377
Sitka, Alaska 99835

Angeles

Alan Carlin, Chairman
627-J San Vicente Blvd.
Santa Monica, California
  90402

Lyle Taylor, Conservation
  Chairman
1434 East Rio Verde Drive
West Covina, California 91790

*East San Gabriel Valley
  Group*
Leonard Bayless, Chairman
8607 South Bright Avenue
Whittier, California 90602

Long Beach Group
Wilson Dresler, Chairman
6027 Carita
Long Beach, California 90808

Orange County Group
Robert N. Wheatley,
  Chairman
1314 Skyline Drive
Fullerton, California 92631

Palos Verdes Group
Dave Jenkins, Chairman
26711 Fond du Lac Road
Palos Verdes Peninsula,
  California 90274

Pasadena Group
Mrs. Mary Ferguson
3800 Latrobe Street
Los Angeles, California 90031

*San Fernando Valley
  Group*
James K. Barnett, Chairman
520 E. University Ave.
Burbank, California 90504

West Los Angeles Group
Murray Rosenthal, Chairman
3467 Inglewood Blvd.
Los Angeles, California 90066

Atlantic

Alfred Forsyth, Chairman
15 LeRoy Place
Chappaqua, N.Y. 10514

George Schindler,
  Conservation Chairman
267 South Street
New Providence, New Jersey
  07974

Connecticut Group
Wilbur W. Squire, Chairman
7 Tyler Lane
Riverside, Conn. 06078

East Pennsylvania Group
Hal Lockwood, Chairman
182 N. Lansdowne Avenue
Lansdowne, Penna. 19050

Finger Lakes Group
John Schwartz, Chairman
308 Turner Place
Ithaca, N.Y. 14850

New York Group
Jeanne Krause, Chairman
58 E. 83rd St.
New York, N.Y. 10028

North Jersey Group
Walter Wells, Chairman
23 Laurel Avenue
Summit, New Jersey 07901

South Jersey Group
Thomas Southerland,
  Chairman
282 Western Way
Princeton, N.J. 08540

Cumberland

W. R. Holstein, Chairman
3307 Pineneedle Lane
Louisville, Ky. 40222

C. A. Schneider, Conservation
  Chairman
1315 Oak Hill Road
Louisville, Kentucky 40213

Grand Canyon

Lester Olin, Chairman
2244 Avenue A
Yuma, Arizona 85364

Elizabeth Barnett,
  Conservation Chairman
6241 East Mescal
Scottsdale, Arizona 85251

Rincon Group
Don Kucera, Chairman
7013 East Kingston Drive
Tucson, Arizona 85710

Great Lakes

Warren R. Dewalt, Chairman
624 Wellner Road
Naperville, Illinois 60540

Mrs. William Meyers,
  Conservation Chairman
1236 Judson Avenue
Evanston, Illinois 60202

Missouri Group
John H. Stade, Chairman
7529 Rowles Avenue
Ferguson, Missouri 63135

Great Lakes (Cont.)

Prairie Group
John R. Bickel, Chairman
1005 South Busey
Urbana, Illinois 61801

Hawaii

Janet Gordon, Chairman
Box 5029
Honolulu, Hawaii 96814

Richard Knobel, Conservation
    Chairman
Box 192
Haleiwa, Hawaii 96712

John Muir

Robert M. Smith, Chairman
119 Monona Avenue
Madison, Wisconsin 53703

Donald Beyer, Conservation
    Chairman
35 Roby Road
Madison, Wisconsin 53705

Kern-Kaweah

Joe Fontaine, Chairman
Star Route
Tehachapi, California 93561

Glenn Beerline, Conservation
    Chairman
Star Route Box 1144
Tehachapi, California 93561

Loma Prieta

Peter Scott, Chairman
1135 North Branciforte
    Avenue
Santa Cruz, California 95060

Olney Smith, Conservation
    Chairman
1919 Adele Place
San Jose, California 95125

Santa Cruz Group
Raynor Talley, Chairman
1979 Jennifer Drive
Aptos, California 95003

Peninsula Regional Group
Bill Freedman, Chairman
40 Terrier
Hillsboro, California 94010

Lone Star

Dr. Aylmer H. Thompson,
    Chairman
Meteorology Department
Texas A & M University
College Station, Texas 77843

Delbert K. Weniger,
    Conservation Chairman
306 Army
San Antonio, Texas 78215

North Texas Group
John Biewener, Chairman
10864 Waterbridge Circle
Dallas, Texas 75218

San Antonio Group
Marvin Baker, Jr., Chairman
Geography Department
Trinity University
San Antonio, Texas 78212

Austin Group
Dr. Daniel E. Willard,
  Chairman
5906 Sierra Madre
Austin, Texas 78751

Houston Group
Paul W. Hull, Chairman
4533 Braeburn
Bellair, Texas 77401

New Orleans Group
William Futrell, Chairman
3323 Jefferson Avenue
New Orleans, Louisiana 70125

Los Padres

Mrs. James Higman,
  Chairman
3408 Cliff Drive
Santa Barbara, California
  93105

Arguello Group
Ellwood S. Pickering,
  Chairman
1200 West Pine
Lompoc, California 93436

Sespe Group
Roland J. Roberts, Chairman
1011 Cadway
Santa Paula, California 93060

Mackinac

Virginia Prentice, Chairman
507 Walnut
Ann Arbor, Michigan 48104

Mrs. E. Leroy Bierke,
  Conservation Chairman
306 West Meadowbrook
Midland, Michigan 48640

Central Michigan Group
Daniel T. Griner, Chairman
343½ South Cochran
Charlotte, Michigan 48813

Mother Lode

Bruce Kennedy, Chairman
1523 5th Street
Sacramento, California 95814

Wayne Ginsburg, Conservation
  Chairman
165 Fourth Street No. 10
Woodland, California 95695

Shasta Group
Dennis Cowan, Chairman
2265 Paris Avenue
Redding, California 96001

Yahi Group
Noble Moore, Chairman
6684 Evergreen Lane
Paradise, California 95969

Yokut Wilderness Group
Ken Dailey, Chairman
161 Drake Avenue
Modesto, California 95350

New England

Roger Marshall, Chairman
33 Linnaen Street
Cambridge, Massachusetts
02138

Maine Group
David Harrison, Chairman
Jackson Laboratory
Bar Harbor, Maine 04609

Western Massachusetts
Stanley Mikelk, Chairman
University of Massachusetts
Amherst, Massachusetts 01002

North Star

Richard Thorpe, Chairman
3460 Wescott Hills Drive
St. Paul, Minnesota 55111

Warren Roska, Conservation
 Chairman
3048 North Lee
Minneapolis, Minnesota 55422

Ohio

Stewart Rowe, Chairman
146 Congress Run Road
Cincinnati, Ohio 45215

Dr. Homer W. McCune,
 Conservation Chairman
580 Larchmont Drive
Cincinnati, Ohio 45215

Cleveland Group
A. H. McClelland, Chairman
4900 Beachwood Drive
Sheffield, Ohio 44054

Pacific Northwest

Mrs. Richard M. Noyes,
 Chairman and Conservation
 Chairman
2014 Elk Avenue
Eugene, Oregon 97403

British Columbia Group
Terry Simmons, Chairman
Geography Department
Simon Fraser University
Burnaby 2, British Columbia,
 Canada

Eugene Group
Richard P. Gale, Chairman
2232 McMillan Street
Eugene, Oregon 97405

Columbia Group
Bill Nordstrom, Chairman
2775 Southwest Sherwood
 Drive
Portland, Oregon 97201

Inland Empire Group
Jay Holliday, Jr., Chairman
226B Cleveland
Pullman, Washington 99163

Klamath Group
Garth Keefer, Chairman
P.O. Box 1774
Klamath Falls, Oregon 97601

Puget Sound Group
Mrs. J. C. Powers, Chairman
4905 University Place
 Northeast
Seattle, Washington 98105

Redwood

Sergei Spiridonoff, Chairman
2022 Beverly Way
Santa Rosa, California 95404

John Tuteur, Jr., Conservation
    Chairman
1393 Green Valley Road
Napa, California 94558

Redwood North Group
Mrs. William Vinyard,
    Chairman
Route 1, Box 825
Trinidad, California 95570

Rio Grande

Brant Calkin, Chairman
Route 1, Box 267
Santa Fe, New Mexico 87501

Col. Henry Zeller,
    Conservation Chairman
Route 4, Box 29
Santa Fe, New Mexico 87501

Riverside

George Shipway, Chairman
1327 Toledo Way
Upland, California 91786

Bill Laurie, Conservation
    Chairman
6163 Argyle
San Bernardino, California
    92404

Rocky Mountain

Vincent Arp, Chairman
7837 Vairview Road
Boulder, Colorado 80302

H. Ruckel, Conservation
    Chairman
70 Clarkson Street #9
Denver, Colorado 80218

Boulder Group
Larry Brown, Chairman
3350 Euclid Avenue
Boulder, Colorado 80303

Fort Collins Group
John Barker, Chairman
Box 807 CS Student Center
Fort Collins, Colorado 80521

Casper Group
Joe Green, Chairman
Box 785
Casper, Wyoming 82601

Aspen Group
Mrs. Harold Harvy, Chairman
Box 199
Aspen, Colorado 81611

San Diego

Richard Rypinski, Chairman
1364 Crest Road
Del Mar, California 92014

Philip R. Pryde, Conservation
    Chairman
5420 55th Street #14
San Diego, California 92115

San Francisco Bay

Bill Simmons, Chairman
2700 Russ Building,
San Francisco, California
  95104

Kent E. Watson, Conservation
  Chairman
3779 Harrison Street Apt. 205
Oakland, California 94611

Santa Lucia

Harold Miossi, Chairman
P.O. Box 606
San Luis Obispo, California
  93401

Jesse Arnold, Conservation
  Chairman
P.O. Box 1211
Cambria, California 93428

Southeast

Robert J. Schaefer, Chairman
2700 Que Street, N.W.
  Apt. 115
Washington, D.C. 20007

Seymour Miller, Conservation
  Chairman
5846 21st St., North
Arlington, Virginia 22205

Baltimore Group
Robert Nied, Chairman
2 Pasco Court
Baltimore, Maryland 21208

Blue Ridge Group
Carl J. Holcomb, Chairman
Price Hall VPI
Blacksburg, Virginia 24061

Carolinas Group
Theodore A. Snyder, Jr.,
  Chairman
Box 232
Greenville, South Carolina
  29602

Delaware Group
Dennis Neuzil, Chairman
3 DeKalk Square
Newark, Delaware 19711

Florida Group
J. Kenneth Watson, Chairman
1401 N.W. 30th Street
Gainesville, Florida 32601

Georgia Group
Mary Jane Brock, Chairman
2629 Arden Road Northwest
Atlanta, Georgia 30327

Tehipite

Charles H. Cehrs, Chairman
3035 East Buckingham Way
Fresno, California 93726

George Whitmore,
  Conservation Chairman
Box 485
Kingsburg, California 93631

Merced Group
Charles Ostrander, Chairman
1786 Eucalyptus
Atwater, California 95301

Toiyabe

John Houghton, Chairman
232 Hunter Lake Drive
Reno, Nevada 89502

Irving Pressman, Conservation
   Chairman
111 East 6th
Carson City, Nevada 89701

Las Vegas Group
Howard Booth, Chairman
4224 Chatham Circle #2
Las Vegas, Nevada 89109

Uinta

Mrs. June Viavant, Chairman
676 South 12th East
Salt Lake City, Utah 84102

Jack McLellan, Conservation
   Chairman
2459 East 6600 South
Salt Lake City, Utah 84121

Ventana

Roy E. Anderson, Chairman
Box 1288
Salinas, California 93901

James S. Demetry,
   Conservation Chairman
1441 Via Marettino
Monterey, California 93940

SIERRA CLUB FILMS

THE GRAND CANYON. 26 min.; sound and full color.

AN ISLAND IN TIME: The Point Reyes Peninsula (San Francisco, California). 28 min.; sound and full color.

WILDERNESS ALPS OF STEHEKIN (Northern Cascades of Washington). 30 min.; sound and full color.

WASTED WOODS. 15 min.; sound and color.

GLEN CANYON (Dam on Colorado River). 29 min.; sound and full color.

TWO YOSEMITES. 10 min.; sound and full color.

NATURE NEXT DOOR (Children discover wild creatures). 28 min.

WILDERNESS RIVER TRAIL (Dinosaur National Monument, Utah/Colorado). 29 min.; sound and full color.

NO ROOM FOR WILDERNESS? (Population explosion). 28 min.; sound and full color.

THE REDWOODS (1968 Academy Award winner). 30 min.; sound and full color.

These films may be ordered from Association Films at 600 Grand Avenue, Ridgefield, New Jersey 07657; phone 201 943-8200. Rental: $5.00.